What People Are

Storytelling

Beautifully written by an enchanting storyteller. Halo Quin provides the structure for the reader to map out their own story and enables them to entwine the narrative within their own lives. Words have power, words have magic, and this book will show you how to weave them into something quite wonderful.
Rachel Patterson, witch, podcast host and author of more than 25 books about witchcraft, including *Witchcraft into the Wilds*, *Beneath the Moon*, and the *Kitchen Witchcraft* series.

This is an ideal book for anyone starting out on the bard path. It has a great deal to offer anyone exploring ritual or who wants to develop their ritual skills, regardless of path. There are some great tools on offer here for growing as a performer and enhancing your spiritual work. Highly recommended.
Nimue Brown, ritual leader, Druid, prolific performer, and author of both fiction and non-fiction including *Pagan Dreaming*, *Druidry and the Ancestors*, and *Beyond Sustainability*.

Storytelling for Magic

Bardic Skills and Ritual-Craft for
Witches and Pagans

Storytelling for Magic

Bardic Skills and Ritual-Craft for Witches and Pagans

Halo Quin

**MOON
BOOKS**

London, UK
Washington, DC, USA

CollectiveInk

First published by Moon Books, 2025
Moon Books is an imprint of Collective Ink Ltd.,
Unit 11, Shepperton House, 89 Shepperton Road, London, N1 3DF
office@collectiveinkbooks.com
www.collectiveinkbooks.com
www.moon-books.net

For distributor details and how to order please visit the 'Ordering' section on our website.

Text copyright: Halo Quin 2024

ISBN: 978 1 80341 406 5
978 1 80341 407 2 (ebook)
Library of Congress Control Number: 2024931777

A CIP catalogue record for this book is available from the British Library.

Design: Lapiz Digital Services

UK: Printed and bound by CPI Group (UK) Ltd, Croydon, CR0 4YY
Printed in North America by CPI GPS partners

We operate a distinctive and ethical publishing philosophy in all areas of our business, from our global network of authors to production and worldwide distribution.

Contents

Greetings from the Storyteller   xi

Introduction   1

Chapter 1.   The Magic of the Voice   5

Chapter 2.   The Power of Stories   17

Chapter 3.   Archetypes, Deities, and Stories of
the Land   27

Chapter 4.   The Bard's Craft – How to Learn
a Story   38

Chapter 5.   The Bard's Craft – How to Tell a Story   45

Chapter 6.   The Craft of Ritual   56

Chapter 7.   From Myth to Magic   64

Chapter 8.   Storytelling Skills in Magic   78

Chapter 9.   Next Steps   83

Appendix 1.   Foundational Magic Skills   88

Appendix 2.   Gods and Spirits   92

Appendix 3.   The Birth of Taliesin   94

Appendix 4.   Recommended Reading   96

About Halo Quin   97

Previous Titles

Your Faery Heart
B00932SH6U

Pixie Kisses
978-1447523444

Pagan Portals – Your Faery Magic
978-1785350764

Pagan Portals – Gods and Goddesses of Wales
978-1785356216

Twisted – Honest Reflections of a Kinky Witch
978-1916339644

All That Glitters – Wonderings & Wanderings of a Changeling Bard
978-1916339651

Pagan Portals – Folktales, Faeries, and Spirits
978-1-78535-941-5

Crimson Craft – Sexual Magic for the Solo Witch
978-1-78535-939-2

To Taliesin, who lights my bardic path.
To the bards, skalds, and storytellers of old, who weave magic with their words still, spinning the threads of history into the future. May we walk in your footsteps and share our stories in honour of the gods, and for the good of all beings.
To my Mum, who always listens to my tales.
And to Steve, who supports me from behind the scenes and reminds me to be my big, leonine self.

Greetings from the Storyteller

Hello my lovely readers!

In your hands you hold the keys to bringing the powerful magic of those ancient magic-weavers, the storytellers, into your life.

This book is a guide to using the skills of the bard in your rituals to enhance your magic, whether crafting spells on your own, or performing ritual for a crowd. In these pages you will learn how to use your voice in magic, how to unravel the secrets of stories, how to craft your own rituals to bring the power of myths and folk tales into your life, and how to find, learn, and tell stories that enchant your audience.

I am both a professional storyteller and a ritualist, and I first learned how powerful storytelling could be in Reclaiming Witchcraft Tradition rituals, and at the pagan celebrations at Avebury. I apprenticed as a bard in an Iron Age roundhouse in Wales sharing the myths round a smoky fire, with adults and children crowded round to listen to the old tales of gods and heroes. Thank you to my first bardic mentor, and friend, the archaeologist nicknamed "Dark Necromancer" by King Arthur, Brochfael (now there's a tale for another time). Since then, I have attended and hosted storytelling circles where I have learned from many, including Milly Jackdaw and Peter Stevenson who regularly support and inspire my work, honed my craft, and told to audiences numbering from one to a hundred or more, and everything in between.

Over the years I have found that stories, whether shared in a ritual setting or a bustling market, carry magic that connects us back to our past, and forward to the future, all while enchanting the now and bringing us closer to the magical powers we hold dear, the deities, archetypes, spirits and energies who we come to know better through their tales.

We can learn magic through stories, we can meet our deities through stories, and we can heal ourselves through stories.

By sharing them we also share that magic, connection, and healing with those around us. Stories live through the telling of them and this is how they weave the much needed magic of connection and understanding through the world. In short; the world needs storytellers.

Perhaps you picked up this book thinking you'd never be brave enough to tell anyone else a story, and there's plenty of magic in these pages for you if that isn't your path. And, even so, I'd like to invite you to just gently hold the thought that we humans have told stories for as long as we have had language. Storytelling can be as simple as telling a friend; "oh, I heard a tale I really loved, which went something like…"

One reason storytelling is so powerful is that narrative is part of how we communicate, make, and share our understanding of the world. Thus, as you learn more stories you will expand your understanding of what is possible, and as you deepen your skills in sharing them, you strengthen your ability to change your life, and thus, the world.

Welcome to the world of storytelling as magic, and storytelling for magic. I can't wait to hear the stories you choose to share!

In delight,
~Halo Quin

Introduction

In an ideal world I'd invite you along to our local storytelling circle, in a cosy bookshop tucked away by the sea, to show you the magic of storytelling. Or we'd meet round a fire at a festival and swap tales deep into the night. We'd weave myth-soaked ritual together in fields and forests and halls, as the moon rose high in the sky, or the sun warmed our skin.

You never know, maybe one day we will. For now, here is a book you can put in your pocket and turn to as often as you like.

I've always found books to be magical anyway. They carry words across time and space, so I can speak to you in my future, your now. This is my offering to magical folk who love stories, whether you're a Druid, a Witch, a Magician, a Pagan... or even a Bard yourself, I hope you'll find some inspiration, some *Awen*, in these pages.

How to Use This Book

This is a workbook, designed to be worked through from beginning to end as later exercises will build on earlier ones, but you are, of course, very welcome to dip in and out and follow your curiosity!

I've written this for pagans and other magical folk who would like to bring the bardic art of storytelling into your practice, so I expect you've already got some magical skills under your belt but I've included some basic magical practices in Appendix 1 for you, in case you're just starting out.

Keep a Journal

Use a notebook or folder to record your journey. Keep notes of the techniques you find most helpful, stories you find, responses you have to the exercises. Record how you feel about your explorations, what works for you and what doesn't, and what you most want to improve on next.

Make This Book Yours!

I know it is controversial, but I very much encourage you to make notes in the margins, to highlight useful pieces, and include your thoughts and comments in the pages of this book so you can see how your storytelling journey evolves over time. Make this book useful to you! And if you don't fancy writing on the pages (even in pencil) then sticky-notes are a wonderful tool.

Alternatively... keep these notes in your journal!

Start a Folder of Stories

As you find stories that you love, write or print them out and keep them in your folder with notes as to where you found them and who told or wrote the version you've got. Wherever possible it is best to give credit for who you learned the story from, whether an author or a storyteller.

It's up to you whether you organise your stories by theme, by title, by country, or something else. I keep an index of titles in my folder, which helps me remember what stories I've learned and where to find them when I want to revise them or check a detail, name, or credit.

Note: stories in song form absolutely count! We won't be looking at them specifically in this book but if you love them, collect them! Do check out the copyright laws in your country around the recording and sharing of music, however, as these can get tricky. On the same note, copyright laws also apply to modern stories, and the unique plotlines of films, novels, and so on, so look for traditional folk tales, myths and legends, and older tales within the oral tradition, and the original versions of stories that you want to tell. You can practice learning and telling any tale that you choose, however, just keep those modern ones for private spaces, or get permission from the creator for how you want to share their work.

Consider a Recording Device

It can be helpful to practice stories with a recording device as it feels a little bit more like having an audience and, if you're ADHD like me or otherwise easily distracted, it can help with staying focused on the task when there isn't another person to keep you accountable. It also gives you the opportunity to listen back and check which bits you like, and which parts you'd like to change.

Do the Exercises

It is very tempting to just read a book cover to cover and not actually put any of the techniques in it into practice, but storytelling is a verb, a doing, not just a knowing.

I'm very much in favour of magic as practice, so throughout this book will be exercises to play with, and I do mean play. This is a part of magic where you can, and should, let your inner child out to explore. Your inner child is the part of you that never forgot how wonder-filled and magical the world can be, and how powerful play is in itself.

Accessibility – Adapt Everything for You

It's up to you to take these practices and make them yours. Some will resonate and some won't. Some may be out of your comfort zone, or range of ability, and I trust that you'll know best how to adapt things to suit you. I'll always try to give alternatives but do apply your common sense and your wonderful creative skills to play with them.

Storytelling is often considered to be an oral tradition, and that is our primary focus here, but at its heart it is about language in the moment as art, and this can be a language of image, such as paper puppets, or gesture, such as traditional dances from India or sign language, or vocalised words, or methods using AAC ("Augmentative and Alternative Communication" — strategies and tools for those that may struggle with speech). I've included some suggestions for adaptations in the exercises, but you know yourself and your communication methods best so please do take the suggestions here and play with them. Ask yourself: how might these principles apply to you?

Focus on Principles

As you'll find in these pages, I have endeavoured to give the reasons why I've suggested certain exercises or methods, and this is so you can learn the principles behind the techniques, and apply them to yourself, your circumstances, and your style. Storytelling, like magic, is such a personal thing that everyone will do it slightly differently. If you pick up some of the principles, you'll be able to take the information and skills offered in this book and make it truly your own.

Have Fun

Enjoy! Storytelling is a natural human expression, and whether you start telling tales yourself or just use the skills within to enhance your magic, this is something to play with. Let your relationship with stories and storytelling unfold and find your own style! The world needs more storytellers, because we are, at heart, storytelling animals, and stories bring us home.

Chapter 1

The Magic of the Voice

I step into the centre of the circle, for tonight is my turn to tell part of the tale. I take a deep breath, drawing up the power of the earth, sweeping my staff round to gather in the waiting witches. There is a moment of stillness, of silence, as we wait together for that first word to move from potential into expression... for the enchantment to begin. I feel silence of listening itself calling to the Divine Inspiration we call Awen...

Invoking the Bard

Imagine, just for a moment, that you're sat around a fire with a fabulous storyteller. They may have been speaking, singing, or weaving their story with music, but you are listening, deeply and utterly immersed in the world of the tale. You have followed the wolf through the deep dark forest, witnessed a goddess claim her wings from the depths of despair, and heard the very music of Pan's pipes calling you onward.

As the story comes to an end you emerge, blinking, to a moment of silence. All around you there are others, also slowly coming back to themselves. After a moment someone realizes that the tale world has returned you all to where you began and they break the spell by clapping in appreciation. The noise dispels the last of the enchantment and you all join in, smiling, wiping away a tear, re-remembering where you are.

But something is different. The story itself reflected part of your life and, somehow, by following the hero's adventure you faced that challenge you'd been carrying. The wolf meets you in your dreams, the forest welcomes you home, something in you has changed. It might be subtle, it might take time to be felt fully, but the spell of the story has enchanted you and left you better than you were before.

This is the magic of story.

This is the enchantment of the bardic arts.

And this is a power that can be brought into any magical act to enhance it, to bring a group together, to invoke the magic desired, and to fundamentally change the world.

Our Adventure...

As a witch and a performer, I've always been fascinated by how art and magic intertwine, and how closely related performance and ritual are. In a nutshell (why not an eggshell? What kind of nut? But I digress...) this is because the human animal is a sensual creature, and art is the language of the senses. Symbols, colours, rhythm, music, narrative, movement, beauty, wonder, and all the sensory and emotive delights all entice us in and speak to our deep selves. Narrative has a hypnotic effect, calming our conscious, chattering worries and guiding our powerful, magical subconscious in healing and transforming. Beauty relaxes us, wraps us in its arms and lifts our spirits, empowering us to engage in the magic of magic. And experiencing the confidence of someone leading a ritual, acting *as if* they were indeed the powerful priestess they are magically, allows us to open to possibility with trust. When the outward expression reflects the inner power, it helps us find our way to the deeper places more easily.

And it's fun.

All these things are tools that can be used within our magical practice, whether we are casting a spell in the privacy of our bedroom or leading a gathering atop Glastonbury Tor. There are practical skills that can be used to support our magic, and artistic concepts that can be applied, even by those of us who do not consider ourselves to be creative at all!

If you needed another reason to explore this magical thread, then these are also ways of engaging with magical energies which underly a lot of Western magical practice, including modern paganism, and elsewhere too.

The Bard and the Awen

The Bard, the Skald, the Poet; by whatever name these magical figures are known to weave magic. Specifically, these magicians weave magic with their words. Often spoken or sung, sometimes written, their power is such that they were thought to be able to change the luck of a battle, bring healing and immortality, and to lay low with a curse, just with a few well-chosen sounds. Taliesin (Welsh), Orpheus (Greek), William Shakespeare (English), Bragi (Norse); all recognized as skilled wordsmiths who changed the world of their audience. Just as magicians find magic words in their grimoires, bards transform all language into magic. But how?

In the stories, this skill is often given to the bard from divine sources. Taliesin, for example, acquired "the Awen" (Divine Inspiration) through an apparent accident after his year and a day stirring the cauldron of the goddess and witch, Ceridwen. In Greek mythology, the muses grant their artistic devotees inspiration and the divine spark of genius that makes their art sing. In Norse mythology Odin worked hard to get close enough to earn a sip of the mead of inspiration from a giant, and then carried all of it back to the gods, dripping some of it into the land of humans. The magic in the music and the words, then, comes from a union between devotion and the divine. In Folklore, particularly skilled musicians may be said to have been blessed with their ability to enchant an audience by the Faery Queen herself.

The bard puts in the work to develop their skills and make space for the fire of inspiration, and the divine muse pours through them.

Within the *Order of Bards, Ovates, and Druids* (OBOD) all members begin as bards because the language, stories, and patterns we learn give us a foundation for everything that comes after. Within the witchcraft tradition of Reclaiming, a tradition known for its powerful and creative rituals, ritualists often work with stories and myths in our rituals because they hold keys to magical secrets, and by going on a journey through the story with the protagonist we transform ourselves, and the world.

Within these pages, then, you will find tools for magic, and practices to develop your bardic skills through the art of storytelling. This is a practical book for helping you connect to the otherworldly and divine inspiration that is the source of all magic, and then to bring it into the world through ritual, intention, and story,

Spell Craft – the Magic of Language

The magic of language is understood even in non-pagan circles. If we explore hypnotism, we can find theories about how rhythm and imagery in language support our transition into alternative states of consciousness — i.e. trance. Within psychology, especially Jungian psychoanalysis, we find the patterns of stories and "characters" known as archetypes describing our inner world, and working with those can help us shift them and heal them. And in "Neuro-Linguistic Programming" (NLP) practitioners talk about how we can use language to program our minds.

All of these aspects are seen, in practice, in the dance of poetry, song, and story. But it is so much more than "all in our heads", the bardic practices work on these levels AND, as you'll see if you haven't experienced it already, the magic ripples out through all the energetic realms to cause transformation and healing beyond our own internal worlds. This all begins with our words.

Words are vibrations. The whole universe is vibrations. So, it stands to reason that speaking words can change the vibrations of what is. When we speak with intention, we take responsibility in our own lives for changing the vibrations (i.e. everything!) in which we live. The skill of choosing the right words is simpler than it might seem, in many ways, and is one of the skills of the bard which we can use in our magic.

This is easier to do in spaces set aside from our daily lives, where we leave our habits at the door, so that we can then take our new words back into our wider life, so set aside some time for the following practices. You can sit at an altar, light a candle or incense, pour yourself a cuppa in your favourite mug, sit under a tree, or wrap yourself in your favourite blanket. Choose whatever it is that marks this time as dedicated to your magical work for you, and do that now, before working with the exercises in this chapter and the chapters ahead.

Bespelling

Both en-CHANT-ing and SPELL-ing are words that illustrate one major way of creating magic: using our voices and our words.

These can be thought of as bringing magical change in two main ways; firstly, our voices are sound, which is literally vibrations, and utterances change the vibrations around us and in the world. If the world is made of vibrations (atoms, energy, or even the movement of objects), then changing those vibrations changes the world. Magic!

Secondly, the words we choose are both symbols which our subconscious takes as instructions, and patterns which the people around us respond to.

So, we can play with this through affirmations.

Exercise: Affirmations

1. Think of something you desire. (For example, to not be scared during public speaking, such as during a ritual with your friends.)
2. Make it a positive thing — something you want rather than something you don't want. (OK, so... confidence and ease in public speaking.)
3. Now put it into a sentence as a statement, as if it were already true now. (In my example: I have confidence and ease in my public speaking.)

This gives you a traditional affirmation, i.e., "a statement that affirms." You can write this on sticky-notes and keep them on your bathroom mirror, include them on the lock screen of your phone, or in a shortened form as a temporary password (e.g. C0nfidence*Ease), and any other places you can think of that you'll see it often.

Read it aloud every time you see it. This is so you are giving yourself this instruction, like you're programming yourself and the world so that whatever you desire is true now.

Exercise: Beyond Affirmations – Invoking Your Magical Self

Affirmations are useful tools in themselves, but we're going to take it a step further, however, and employ the bardic skills which take this process to the next level of magic efficacy.

1. Take a blank page and write your desire at the top of the page.
2. Read your affirmation aloud a few times, allow yourself to really feel as though it is true. Imagine that it is true, that you really are confident, or strong, or a master

magician, or a fantastic storyteller. Whatever desire you are focusing on. Really imagine what it would feel like.

3. Underneath, begin to write the words and images that come to mind, in any order. Don't censor them, just let them flow onto the page.

4. Fill the page with as many words, images, sensations, feelings, or anything that feels like it fits with your desire.

5. When the page is full, set it aside for a bit and take a break. Go get a cup of your preferred brew (and stir that cup like it is a cauldron of inspiration, blessed by Ceridwen herself) and come back.

6. Look over your list and circle or highlight the words and phrases you really like.

Now you're going to use those to write an invocation of yourself, as the one who has your desire. Don't worry, we'll do it together!

At its simplest, an invocation is a magical invitation, so in this case you're inviting your future self into now (which makes the desire, that that future self has, also here now). So, start with words of invitation:

"I call to you..."

And then you put your affirmation, phrased as though it were a description of someone. For example:

"I call to you, oh confident one, who always speaks with ease!"

Or:

"I invite you to be here now, Halo, Master Storyteller!"

See what I did there? You are invoking yourself, so use your name and a title that appeals to you. And now, using the words and imagery that really resonated, you continue describing your future self, calling them to be present. Remember, you don't have to get it perfect, or to share it with anyone, this is just to play with.

So, I might write something like:

"I call to you, oh confident one!
You who speaks with ease,
whose words are always just what is needed,
and whose stage presence is captivating to your audience!
I invite you, Halo, Master storyteller, to be here with me now!"

Now, when you really look at what I've written, you'll see it's simple and direct. You can use more poetic language, you can make it rhyme, you can even swap out "your" for "thine" and so on if you enjoy the way it sounds. But for now, just notice how simple this can be.

The Power of the Voice

You can perform a spell simply with the written word, but, if you want to change the world magically then that's going to take energy.

Let's talk about energy for a moment.

Both science and magical metaphysics agree: The world we live in is one of energy, of vibrations which we experience as physical, as consciousness, as emotion, as spirit, and so on. Our world is made of vibrations, and every vibration is a sound. The universe in its wholeness is a song of interwoven melodies.

We can find this truth in the name: "uni" — one, "verse" — song.

This song is made of the vibrations of each being and each event, harmonising together into a whole, and every time we make a change, we shift the song. By creating vibrations that carry the melody of our choosing we can change the world by changing the song.

So, the universe is a song, a pattern of vibrations, and if you want to change those vibrations the more you can set energy in motion, the more likely you'll change the tune. Or in other words, the act of *expressing* your written words increases their magical power.

When you're leading in a group ritual you are also inviting those present to lend their energy and intention. Whether you are sharing a seven word statement or a ten minute invocation, the more you can hold the participants' attention, the more your magic weaves together to increase the power in your spell. If you're taking everyone on a journey, internally or astrally, the words become signposts and guides. In all cases they give the listeners — both embodied humans and the gods and spirits who have been invited to join the ritual — guidance on where the energy is and where you are sending it, as well as what story you are telling and what magic you are weaving, so that everyone can keep their conscious mind in alignment with the goal of the moment, which keeps the magic on track.

In these rituals the spoken (or sung) word is an extremely valuable tool, though it is not the only way of expressing words. You might hold a silent ritual, with symbols or written instructions. You might use gesture or sign language to communicate the journey, but these are all forms of expression, transforming the *idea* into *manifest energy* and changing *what is*.

But we'll come back to rituals later. Now we want to take the invocation we've created and transform it into moving energy. We want to *express* it.

Exercise: Many Voices

Weaving together words is an art in itself, and clear communication is important because whoever is hearing the words needs to be able to hear and understand them. And then there's the delivery.

1. Look over what you've written. Read it in your head. How does it feel?
2. Now whisper it, as though you don't want anyone else to hear it. How does that feel?
3. Now whisper it as though you are telling it to the spirits. Or as though it is the most important information you have ever told anyone, but if you speak above a whisper, it'll set off an avalanche. How different is that?
4. Now say it out loud in your normal voice. Then try projecting it, as if across a busy cafe. Then shout it if you can. How do they all feel? Experiment with saying it with different volumes and moods.
5. Finally, pick a note that feels comfortable to chant it in, and remember, you don't have to sing well, this is for magic, not the stage. Imagine that, as you chant it, you are vibrating with the feeling of it being true, it being real, and your voice is vibrating the universe. Explore different pitches until you find something that *feels* right.

Think over how the different ways of saying your invocation felt. Which felt most magical to you? Which felt like the universe was agreeing with you? Which felt the most like you were saying something true?

This is all valuable information for you to use in the rest of your magical practice, with your affirmations, and when you have something important to say. Remember the feelings and consider; in what way are you choosing to enchant the world with your voice?

Exercise: Translating into Written Language

The same principles apply to writing and formatting text. You can use italics, bolds, different line lengths, different typefaces and font sizes, all the shift the way in which you, or other people, read it. You can experiment with colours, shapes, page colour, decorations, word art... anything that you like. Underlying all of this is the way in which we express this information to both ourselves and the wider universe.

Explore the different visual aspects of written language and notice what emotions each evokes for you.

If you have trouble writing, you can use a recording device and play with it all using audio. If you have trouble with audio, you can adapt this to purely written exercise. The same principles should also apply to other forms of communication, but my experience is very much coloured by my abilities. (If you have experience with sign language and other forms of communication, then I'd love to hear how you might adapt this exercise to suit!)

Prioritise Emotion over Complexity

Returning to the simplicity of language in an invocation, then, it can be really useful to keep the words themselves simple and to put more energy into the emotion expressed, the calling and longing and then arrival, of that which is being invoked. Ultimately the words themselves are a vehicle for the magic, and, alongside that, they are themselves ways of shaping and supporting the magic that you are doing. Equally, as you may have felt earlier, the way in which you express the words makes a big difference. Just as the simplest of invocations can become powerful with an emotive, energized reading, so too can a beautiful invocation fall flat when read without care. Combining both is the skill that transforms mere words into bardic magic.

All of these aspects of expression can be used to support your magic and your intention. If you are working within a group then you have an extra layer to consider: can they hear you? In a large group outside, for example, wind can become an issue. You may have deaf members in your group. How might you communicate the intention and imagery in ways that support them being included? We'll be talking about a lot of different modes of expression through this book, but this is an important aspect to start thinking about, especially for wordy folk like myself who default to voice-based communication. What works best for you, in your personal magical practice, and what will work best in larger groups may well differ. Explore, experiment, and play.

Your Bardic Magic

What it boils down to, in the cauldron of your practice, is that the time put in choosing words and learning how to put them together into a pattern that feels pleasing is the devotional act of the bard. The feeling which you put in is your own magic that reaches out to the divine. The light that shimmers through the invocation when you share it, an offering to your divine self and the muses, that is Awen, that is the magic of the Storyteller.

So, we've looked at language in magic, specifically how you might craft the language of a spell via "affirmations", and how we might use our voice in different ways to enhance the enchantment. We can whisper, speak, chant, sing, shout... All of these can shift the energy of our magic. And, likewise, we can write using **bold** or *italics*, in different colours, ALL CAPS, or shapes on the page to mimic these energies in the written word. What happens next?

Well, the words become stories...

Chapter 2

The Power of Stories

*Each word pours into the circle we have cast together,
rippling within the canvas of the ritual yurt. I am carried
along with everyone else, my favourite tale tripping from
my tongue as the pain that had me limping moments
before we arrived disappears in the flow of magic and I
leap, turn, pause, mapping the journey across the land
with my body in the circle, taking everyone with me.*

Stories as Spells

Stories enchant the listener, they bespell the world.

Every story we tell ourselves changes how we see the
world, how we see ourselves. And when we change how we
see ourselves and the world, we change how we act... which
changes the world.

But deeper than that, the words we speak are vibrations,
energy that flows across the land and up to the stars. The stories
are energy that we can hear, re-weaving the tapestry of life.
Transforming the song of the world.

In magic we use our intentions, carried in something that
also holds the energy to match, to choose how we change our
melody line.

Affirmations use the psychological component as well as the
magical one, which is an energy in itself, to carry the intention
into our minds as well as out into the world.

Now, remember a time when you were listening to music
and suddenly someone changed the song. Or you were reading
a story, and someone interrupted with a different topic. That
quick shift from one song or story to another is jarring. This
illustrates something important: you know when you've told

yourself something you wish were true, but it was so far from your experience that you didn't really believe it? When that happens the best way to change your thoughts is to find a step in between, an affirmation you can believe more easily, which is a step in the direction you want to move yourself. In the same way, sometimes our magic needs smaller steps to carry us more smoothly toward our desire. Sometimes the melody needs a step-by-step progression to change the song the amount we long for.

Another way we can support our magic is to find a melody line, a vibration in the world, which is already strong, a different chorus line we can join in with instead of being a solo voice in a choir singing different songs.

We can do this in different ways, using sympathetic magic and symbols or colours that resonate with our new song, our intention, or finding a community who are living the way we want to be so we can join their chorus. And we can also do this by finding a story which outlines the transformation we want to undertake. Myths are powerful stories for this purpose.

By using myths in our rituals we bring the vibrations and patterns of those stories into our magical spaces. We can work with them purely as psychological frameworks, Jungian maps to the psyche, or magical maps to initiation, or we can use the imagery and the patterns that they contain to invoke the journey that they describe in our own lives.

For example, if we find ourselves in a difficult time, where circumstances have plunged us into darkness, we might choose to work with a myth of Persephone, who is usually described as being dragged into the underworld, but who finds her power and sovereignty over her life in that darkness by becoming Queen. Or we might choose to work with the legend of Rhiannon, who is blamed for the disappearance of her child but perseveres until he is returned to her.

The story we choose will depend on which deities and cultures we work most closely with, and it is important to respect the culture from which those stories arise — and to understand as much of the context as we can in order to work with them effectively. Some stories are also not suitable for use in general rituals because of the meaning they have for the people who hold them. Folktales and myths from your homeland or culture are usually a good place to start for this reason.

By tuning into the story we need, we support ourselves through psychological development and we boost our magic using the louder melody of the myth to harmonise our intention with.

So how might you go about finding stories, and then choosing which to work with?

Choosing Stories

Sometimes the witch chooses the story, and sometimes the story chooses the witch. (Though as witches we do tend to write our own stories too!)

Exercise: Your Story

Head to your altar, light your candle, or stir your cuppa and settle into your magical space again in the way you've chosen. Turn to a new page, or audio track if you prefer, and begin to make notes on an aspect of your life, starting from when you were born, as though you were writing the outline of a folktale.

Note down the answers to these prompts — use the questions to help you explore your story. You can make your answers as literal or as imaginative as you choose:

1. *Our main character/hero/heroine/protagonist was born to...*
   Imagine you are a fairytale hero; how would you describe your parents? Poor, wealthy, comfortable, kind, struggling? Where did you live? Were there dragons? Or kindly grandparents? Or a wicked stepparent?

2. *Growing up they always wished...*

   What was your dream as a child? Who did you want to be? What did you want to do?

3. *And then, one day...*

   What happened that changed things? Did you realise something? Did you choose to go on an adventure? Did you give up? Did you decide there was something you wanted more? Did something lucky or unlucky happen?

4. *And so...*

   What happened next? What was the result of the event in number 3? Did you begin to fly into success, or spiral into sadness, or settle into the familiar?

5. *Finally...*

   What came next? Or what do you choose next?

Once you're happy that you've got the main points of this thread of your life noted down, look over it as though it was someone else's story. Can you see patterns in it? An overall shape or repeating challenge?

Does it remind you of a story that you're familiar with?

An Example

Many stories have unhappiness and challenge in them, and this is only part of my story, with the complexities of reality simplified to bring out the themes. While there's magic in it, in some ways this is a very ordinary tale:

Our hero was born to loving parents, in an ordinary sort of life.

Growing up, she was always daydreaming, and wished she could live in a world with magic. And then, one day, she met a ghost!

If ghosts are real, *she thought,* then perhaps magic is real too?

And so, she went to the most magical place she knew — the library — where she found something she'd never even thought to look for: a book of magic! She began learning magic, and seeking out teachers. She longed to write magical books, just like the ones that had helped her find a world of magic. Eventually, a raven led her to Wales, where, of course, she fell in love with a boy.

A beautiful boy who told her lies, and convinced her to ignore her dreams to live in a little house with him.

As time went by she began to pine for the dreams that, between working and housework and helping him with his dreams, she never quite had time for.

Finally, she caught him in his lies, and her heart broke. She picked up her coat and left, ready to swim in a world of magic and dream the dreams of her own again.

One pattern in this could be: Protagonist has a dream and sets off to pursue it. While they're successful, they meet someone who wants to take advantage of them, who distracts them from their journey. Eventually they realise what's happened and escape, returning to the life they choose, older and hopefully wiser for it.

This part of my life reminds me of the Selkie stories, or rather, whenever I read about the selkies, I remember how I felt during those years. Selkies are seal shapeshifters who live in the ocean, and the women become human to dance on the beach under the full moon. They're living their dream, true to their own nature. The most well-known selkie stories have a human man steal a magical sealskin so one cannot return to the water, and the selkie has to stay with him as his house-wife. She eventually finds her sealskin and returns to the ocean.

I have worked with the selkie stories, then, to explore and heal that part of my life when I felt like I'd lost my selkie-skin. Telling the story, meditating on it, singing the (imagined) song of the selkie-woman who misses the ocean, writing poetry and making art from the story are all ways I found helped me to explore these feelings and memories.

I have also worked with it in ritual, making my own selkie skin — a decorated cloth — to magically bring back to myself what I'd given away.

If you look at the patterns in your life and find a story that feels like it speaks to you, then you can explore it creatively as a way of engaging with those energies.

Perhaps in your story there is a monster that you need to get past — can you meet it in meditation and befriend it? Or bind it? Or transform it in some way into something that you can deal with?

Perhaps in your story there is a wicked stepparent, and you carry the damage they did to you as a child (whether intentionally or not) — can you call on Baba Yaga and her fire-filled skulls to break their hold on you? Or journey with a girl named Donkey Skin to find a home in a new inner palace?

Perhaps in your story there is a holy grail that has always been out of reach, and you can make or choose an object to represent it that you can place on your altar... perhaps a cup that you fill with water each day to feed that magic coming to you.

Perhaps you've realised that you were the Big Bad Wolf, and you want to choose a different path and become the protector instead of the hunter, or you see yourself in the farmer that stole the selkie skin, and you need to return it.

Reflect on all the possibilities. Who are you in your story? Who are you in someone else's' story? And what magic might you want to work to help you move through the story of your life, to heal, to step into the next stage, to make things right, or to change the story entirely?

Finding Stories!

If, like me, you grew up in an area without much obvious oral storytelling, then you might know stories from novels and film adaptations — like Disney's animated films. These are very often different to the tales they were based on, and that's absolutely fine! Stories have evolved and been rewritten and reimagined for longer than we have written history. It is definitely worth looking up the "original" versions, however, so you can begin to explore those magical threads and tap into the archetypes and energies behind the modern versions. (Plus it avoids copyright issues!)

If you're not sure where else to find stories, however, then let me remind you of that key to a wide world of wonder which I'm sure you've used for other things.

Head to the library and ask the librarian where the myths and legends live, and where the folk and fairytale collections are. Or search online for "mythology", "folktales", or "fairy tales".

You can choose a culture that you're interested in, such as "Welsh Mythology", or "Greek legends", or archetypes and themes that might call to you such as "folk tales about mothers" or "magical animal stories".

You can also ask — in the library, your local bookshop, or a search engine — for storytellers and storytelling circles in your area. There are currently a lot of storytelling circles which are hosted online as well, which you can access anywhere in the world, and many storytellers put videos up of stories they've told, or discussions about stories, so you can explore them even more deeply.

Read, listen, and watch. Begin collecting stories that you really love, or that make you feel things. Notice what themes you come back to again and again, and notice what styles of stories you most enjoy. This will be a lifelong adventure, so don't worry about finishing this task, it is enough that you have begun!

Exercise: A Story That Resonates

In your magical space, make a list of all the stories that you've fallen in love with, because they feel like home or you have seen yourself in one of the characters. These can be folk tales, fairytales, myths, legends, pop culture stories, or any other kind of tale.

For several years me and some friends taught magic informally with the characters and imagery of the world of *Buffy the Vampire Slayer,* and in chaos magic you'll find plenty of people using pop culture icons in place of deities — Superman as a Sun god, for example. It often surprises people how effective this can be, but these are stories and archetypal characters that hold big themes that speak to us. It is often easier to work magic with myths and folk tales because they are, generally, structured in such a way that they leave space for details that apply to many different people, whereas modern stories often focus more on specific personalities and emotional motivations, and, again, there can definitely be copyright issues if you take it into a public sphere, but if you have a story that you connect strongly with then it is definitely worth exploring!

Exercise: A Story That Challenges

Make another list of all the stories that resonate, but that you find challenging. You're not looking for something that triggers a trauma response, or a genre that upsets you, but rather stories that make you reconsider your thoughts on something.

As an example: In one tale of Frau Holla, a mother is cruel to one daughter and indulges the other. The one daughter works hard and ends up gaining riches, whereas the spoiled daughter is rude and ends up covered in tar. This story might resonate with you, or you might find it challenging because you're a parent and you're worried that being "too soft" on your child will spoil them, or, conversely, you might find it difficult because you feel for the hard working child, and it seems as if the story is saying that children treated badly end up doing better in the long run. Or you might find it challenging that the "reward" is financial. Or you might not find it challenging at all.

Nowadays there are many "feminist retellings" of old folk tales, written to make the main (female) characters stronger by today's standards. This is, I think, wonderful and necessary... and there might still be useful magical lessons in the stories that are less comfortable. I tell a version of the tale of Little Red Riding Hood where she is a secret werewolf who scares away the Big Bad Wolf herself, but perhaps when she is rescued by the Woodsman, we see that sometimes it is OK to allow ourselves to be helped when we've gotten into a bad situation. There are many lessons to uncover in stories.

And sometimes the old stories contain some really horrendous things, so I invite you to use your discernment on which pieces to explore!

Reflect on your list of stories and consider what about them you might find challenging.

Which parts feel uncomfortable? On first reflection, why do they make you uncomfortable? On second thought, what wisdom might they have for you that you find difficult to hear?

Exercise: A Different Story to Explore

Visit your library, local bookshop, nearby storytelling circle, or internet search engine and look for collections of folk tales, myths, and legends. Read or listen to the stories you don't already know. Make notes of the ones that you are curious about. Add any that resonate or challenge to your other lists, but include here stories that don't feel close to you and your life, but that intrigue you anyway. Choose one that feels like it might be useful to work with. Ask yourself:

- Why does this intrigue me?
- What about it would I like to bring more of into my life?
- Which bits feel familiar?
- Which bits feel different?

Exercise: Which Story Will You Choose?

Revisit your lists. Which story jumps out at you right now? Which story holds the journey that you feel like you would like to go on, or have been on and would like to explore or heal from? Choose one to begin with.

If this is a traditional story I highly recommend listening to and reading different versions to find the one that you are happiest with. If you can find storytellers — online or in person — to listen to different tellings then that can be a wonderful way of meeting the story through different perspectives.

Chapter 3

Archetypes, Deities, and Stories of the Land

As we race across the land of the story, I feel Her presence flowing round. I am Him, leaping and dancing. I am carrying the wisdom of the old ways, wrapped in Her cloak of magic. Each word is an offering of breath and love, given up in service of my gods, in honour of the land. The witches listening round share in the meeting and together we learn a little more about the beings that guide us, a chance to move closer and meet them themselves.

Archetypes

The same process of working with stories to explore energies and parts of your life also applies to archetypes. Archetypes are Anthropomorphic (human-shaped) ideas of energies and roles that exist in the world. They embody the *idealised* version of that type of person. For example, the Archetypal Writer is always writing, always working on their craft, always coming up with ideas and putting them on paper. A real writer could never actually be like that because they need to eat and sleep, even if they work as a writer full time and write as their hobby as well! We will often take on those roles and energies to some degree, however, and so we can explore archetypes through the roles we take on. Remember to mark your magical space however you choose for each exercise.

Exercise: Exploring Archetypes
First, let's start with exploring different roles that you might find in your life. Get out your journal and put your name in

the centre of an empty page. In the corners of the page, put the cardinal directions: North, East, South, West.

- In the North, write: Work.
- In the East write: Expanding.
- In the South write: Play.
- In the West write: Relationship.

Think about all of the roles you are playing or have played in your life.

Begin to write these around your name in a mind map, see which ones fit under each category.

Some might fit under more than one space, it's up to you where you put them. For Work you might put career roles you've taken, such as 'writer', 'cashier', 'volunteer'. For Expanding it might include roles from school where you were learning new things, or hobbies that you spend time developing yourself, or areas that you are working on self-improvement, such as 'student', 'ritualist', or 'painter'. For Play choose those roles which bring you joy, or that you take for the sheer fun of them, e.g. 'clown', 'bookworm', 'cryptozoologist'. For Relationships think about all the roles and labels people in your life might view you through, which might include 'sibling', 'friend', and 'arch-nemesis' (hopefully not that one!).

Next, when you're ready, turn to a fresh page and write 'Archetypes' in the centre.

In the corners of the page write:

- North/Work
- East/Expanding
- South/Play
- West/Relationship

Now begin to think of all the types of people and roles that might fit on that page. If they don't fit tidily under a particular corner then put them nearer the centre. Use your own roles for inspiration, and you might look tarot cards, or at the roles that deities or mythological characters play — such as 'The Fool', 'The Guide', 'The Parent', 'The Adventurer', 'The Wizard' and so on.

Once you've got a whole bunch, look at the two pages, what do you notice? Do you see some of the roles you take in your life in the archetypes? Do you see archetypes that you definitely are not? Which archetypes would you like to embody in your life but don't quite yet? Which archetypes do you notice are missing, that you had entirely forgotten about?

Exercise: Magic with Archetypes

Now you've had a chance to explore different types of Archetypes, and reflected on which ones you embody, and which ones you'd like to, you can bring them into your magic to start inviting more of that energy into your life.

Choose one Archetype that has qualities you'd like in your life. Perhaps you feel like you need more confidence in using your voice, and 'The Messenger' feels like they might be good at speaking up to you.

Find a story or myth which includes a character who embodies your archetype, in this case; The Messenger.

- Who is in that role?
- What do they do?
- What qualities do they have that make them good at communication?
- What wisdom do they have that might be helpful to you?

Decide if you'd like to meet them and ask them to work with you.

If not, think about who you might like to meet more and choose again.

If so, get comfortable and compose a short invocation for the archetype, and the qualities you're looking for, using the techniques in Chapter 1. It might be as simple as:

"I call to The Messenger, who knows how to speak the Truth clearly and with ease. Join me now."

Once you've got your invocation, begin the imaginative exercise below.

One little reminder — adjust this (and all other exercises in this book) to suit you. 'Imagination' isn't just visual, so when I say 'imagine' you can use whichever sense is best for you — perhaps you hear or feel things more clearly than you see them, that's ok, let the information come to you in the way that makes sense to you.

Meeting the Archetype

1. Settle into your space, make sure you are comfortable and will be undisturbed (turn off the phone, close your door, whatever you need)
2. Take some nice breaths, gradually allowing yourself to breathe slower and deeper, until you feel like you've found a relaxing pace.
3. Feel your body resting on the earth, supported by it.
4. And release any tension, any thoughts from the day, as you breathe and rest, here and now.
5. Now imagine yourself surrounded by a beautiful protective light, you can feel it, or see it, or hear it, or simply know it is there.
6. Let the light of protection grow stronger until you are bathed in it.

7. Into the space you have made, think over the story that your Archetype is in. Think about their part of the story. You can re-read it now if you like, or just remember what you can. Begin to allow a sense of them to build up in this space.

8. Now say your invocation, like you really mean it, as an invitation to the Archetype that that character embodies.

9. Notice how you feel. Imagine the archetype you are calling on coming into your space.

10. What do they look like, sound like, feel like, smell like. What do you notice.

11. Imagine you're having a conversation with them. Introduce yourself, tell them you'd like to learn from them.

12. You might choose to ask them *how you can bring their qualities into your life* or *what wisdom they have for you,* or you may have other questions.

13. Ask your questions, and then listen for the response. Take a breath and allow yourself to soften, to relax, and let yourself be in a receptive state. The answer may come in words or images or a knowing, or any other way. Notice what arises.

14. When you feel like it's time to stop, thank them and say farewell.

15. Let them fade or leave the space.

16. Become aware of the protective light around you, and let your awareness of it relax, like it is fading from view.

17. Come back to where you began, take a nice breath, stretch, feel your body resting upon the earth, and be back in the here and now.

18. Make any notes you need to make, and then go do something mundane to allow the experience to settle into you.

Myths, Legends, and Devotion

Myths are a wonderful way of getting to know deities and other spirits, as well as exploring archetypes, and you can find practices that apply to meeting spirit beings through stories, in relation to working with The Fair Folk, in my book *Folktales, Faeries, and Spirits,* (Moon Books, 2022), but here are some easy ways of meeting your deities and bringing their stories into your magic with them.

Firstly, you can explore the myths in the same way as we did for meeting Archetypes, and use the stories to get to know the deity. By reading about their adventures, you can get to know their personality, likes and dislikes, family and friends, and what they like to help out with in magic.

Reading their stories, or listening to a good storyteller tell them, also gives you different perspectives on how people have related to that deity, and the things that they embody, throughout time. For example, in the oldest stories we have, Eros was born before many of the other gods, a primordial power of Love. Later he became Aphrodite's son. And still later, he was connected to the Roman Cupid, who we often now know as the little cherub on Saint Valentine's Day cards! So once upon a time, Eros — the power of divine, passionate Love, was known to be one of the most powerful forces in the world. Later, he became the child of beauty, and later still, he, and love, is seen as something sweet, even if it still has a little sting in the sharp tipped arrows. So today, when people write about Eros, they might write about his power, or his love for Psyche (the Soul), or about his mischievousness, and it's up to you to explore and feel what your relationship with him might be.

You can repeat the **Meeting the Archetypes** exercise above to meet the deity, based on the story you've chosen to connect with them through, using their nature and mood in the story to invite in that aspect of them.

You can use the information in those stories to gather information on their symbols and build an altar or shrine for them with those objects, scents, and sounds, to give them a space in your world where you can connect with them.

You can choose sections of the stories to read aloud in their honour, as invocations or as devotions. Or you can create a ritual that works with their story to go on a journey with them, and we'll explore this with Ceridwen in Chapter 7.

Seasonal Stories of the Land

In modern pagan circles we often use stories to provide an archetypal thread throughout the year, guiding our relationship to different times. In Wicca there is the story of the fertile Goddess and the dying and reborn God (her consort). There is the modern myth, inspired by older tales, of the Holly and Oak Kings that fight at summer and winter Solstices to rule over half the year each, and the triple faced lady of the moon (with a fourth, hidden face, of course) tells us about the lunar cycles. We have stories about the movement of the land and the seasons (based in Western European cycles, usually). And so on. Each of these can provide a map to transformation, growth, strength, healing, and enchantment. They are most effective, however, when they reflect the shifts in the landscape and the world around us. Transplanting the Holly and Oak kings into land at the equator, or the Arctic circle, will not tell you about the life and magical seasons of the land there. But they might hold keys to an inner process that you're going through, so you get to reflect, discern, consider the context, and decide for yourself.

Remember that stories aren't necessarily fictions or myths, they can be the descriptions of what is physically happening in the land and sky. The stories of the modern pagan wheel of the year are stories of celebration and connection with the land and the cycles of the year. Some groups work with the anthropomorphic stories above, to connect with the energies in human-like forms, and some groups work with the stories of the plants, or the stars in the sky, or myths and legends that resonate for them.

These stories, in ritual, help us to tune into the "melody" of the land and the sky, the cycles of the world. They help us mark the passing of time, and remind us to reflect on our journey, our relationship to the natural world, and our communities. Let's briefly look at the "story" of the Wheel of the Year, in terms of the landscape of Britain, where this was first rooted in this form, and a little astrology. The Wheel of the Year as we know it today is a relatively modern invention inspired by older traditions and festivals, rather than ancient in origin, but it works well for most pagans. Remember, however, that your landscape may well have a different story, and all the dates can vary depending on how you calculate them, and the year, but I'll give the standard versions here.

At Imbolc, around the first of February, the snowdrops begin to emerge through the frost. Life is returning to the land, despite the cold. The first lambs are being born and there is hope in the air, which will carry us through to the spring. Life has survived the worst of the winter, and the light is growing. In astrology, Aquarius rules this time, with inspired thoughts and a breath of fresh, if cold, possibility.

At the Spring Equinox, around 21st March, the days and nights are of equal length. The daffodils blossom, bright yellow and green bringing joy. There might be storms, but there is also warmth, and life begins its turn outward.

At Beltane, around the first of May, the Hawthorn blossoms. The trees are pollinating, the bees are buzzing, and the everyone is in high spirits. We can travel with the daylight, enjoy the land, and sex is in the air. Taurus, the sensual sign of luxury, pleasure, nourishment, and persistence holds the energy here, reminding life to really revel in being embodied.

At the Summer Solstice, around 21st June, the land is abundantly green with life, the sun reaches its peak, and we are blessed with the strength of that moment of stillness, before the agricultural work of the harvest begins.

At Lughnasadh, around the first of August, the grain harvest arrives. The land turns golden under the late summer sun, the heat drying everything out — if we're lucky — preserving the bounty of the land for the winter months to come. Leo the lion rules here. The sign of fire, creativity, confidence, and leadership. This is a time for leading by example and sharing with a big heart. Everyone pitches in to help. Everyone steps up to be their best self and get the work done so the whole community can survive.

At the Autumn Equinox, around 21st September, days and nights balance again, tipping toward longer nights, and the second harvest, of fruit and roots, apples and potatoes. The beings of the land are storing up what they need too, so this is a time of gathering in, and taking stock. What needs doing in preparation for the next steps.

At Samhain, around 31st October (connecting it with Halloween), the cold sweeps across the land, the leaves fall, and the bones of the trees point to the darkening sky. The ancestors feel closer as our attention turns inward, and the final harvest, the culling of the animals that won't last the winter, a sacrifice to sustain the living, happens now. Ruled by Scorpio, this is a time of mystery, of the primal powers of life and death.

At the Winter Solstice, around 21st December, we find the longest night and the shortest day. The land is cold and what life is left hides beneath the surface, waiting. The trees are bare, and people hold a feast to lift their spirits for the coldest part to come.

The *Wheel of the Year* can offer one story, or several, which might reflect the energy you are tuning into, and is a story itself that brings us closer to the rhythms of the landscape, particularly if we align it with what the land we are on is actually doing.

Exercise: Where Are You in the Story?

Reading over the above steps of the story of the land, reflect on where in that cycle the land you are on right now is. Is it bursting into life and pleasure, or is it gathering in time?

Reflect on your own life; are you in a period of stepping up in community and engaging with the hard work of harvesting the seeds you've planted previously? Or are you dreaming of what is to come?

Which part of the Wheel of the Year story are you in now emotionally? Mentally? These may or may not match with what the land is doing, just notice what is true for you now.

Once you've reflected on what is true, take a look at the patterns of your landscape in relation to the calendar. Does the grain harvest happen at the start of August, or September, or February? When is the year at its darkest? When does new life appear?

You can also bring in stories and information from other magical practices here, for example: in Western Astrology the Sun is considered to be "in Scorpio" across the world during late October and early November (this is different in Indian Astrology, and other models, so if you work with those please feel free to adjust the dates for this example!) but where in Britain, Samhain is very definitely in Scorpio season, in Australia it is Beltane that falls at this time. So what is happening in the sky for you? What are the stories here?

What myths and legends do you associate with different times of the year? You might look up the Greek myths of the Zodiac signs, or Norse myths set at specific times, or Welsh myths that describe how particular events happen, and so on.

Begin to collect stories that reflect your sky, and your landscape and the turning seasons where you live, stories of time and change and the relationship between humanity and the earth. Consider what these stories might be saying about your inner landscape. What might they suggest for how to engage with healing the inner and outer environments which shape your life?

Your Story Book

By now you will hopefully have begun collecting stories, including myths, legends, folk and fairy tales, and your own reflections on the land, sky, seasons, and your life. Traditionally a bard wouldn't have kept their tales written down, but nowadays there is much more information flying around to keep track of, and the written word is much more accessible, so keeping records of the stories you collect is a wonderful way of supporting yourself on this journey. Now, however, you're going to tackle that all-important step for telling a tale from memory: learning a story to tell.

Chapter 4

The Bard's Craft – How to Learn a Story

There's no script for this, the story happens anew each time. I could have used my theatre training, laid out every phrase and committed them whole, precise and perfectly formed, to memory, but instead I embraced that balance of memory and inspiration that is the storyteller's art. Each step in the story is a step through the story's world. I travel from point to point, tale anchored in my spirit as tangible places etched on the imaginative layer of the astral. I cannot be complacent, full presence is essential to receive the inspiration that flows through. I am a guide, leading the listening witches from landmark to landmark, and together we experience the story again.

The Magic of Memory

Storytelling in ritual can serve several purposes:

- To set up the magic that you are doing.
- To invoke specific energies and deities or archetypes into the space.
- To relax people and help them shift into a magical state of consciousness.
- To connect everyone to our storytelling ancestors.
- To guide people on a journey through experiences outlined in the story.

And these hold true whether it is just you alone, telling stories to yourself and the spirits, or a large group of people! So, when you tell stories in ritual it is really important to know them well enough that you tell them smoothly.

You can read them from a page, but telling them from memory makes it easier to adjust the story for the time, purpose, and listeners as you can add or remove details as necessary. It also helps to know them well even if you are reading them, so you can really feel what you are reading, rather than concentrating on the reading aspect. Finally, telling stories from memory makes it easier to adapt them for the magic you are doing because you can, as you will see, change the emphasis and invoke different energies with tiny adjustments to the tale.

One of the primary skills of the bard is therefore *memory*, and one of the questions I get asked the most by people who want to tell stories but have yet to begin is how to remember so much. The secret is not to try to *remember* it all consciously, your deep self can hold so much more than your everyday mind. Learn the bones and let the magic help you reweave the rest. Here's how.

Learning the Bones

I begin with a blank sheet of paper.

My biggest struggle is usually remembering the names, so I'll write those at the top, along with their role/archetype if it isn't clear.

Next, I write the key places, in order of appearance.

And then I write the main actions — what happens and where, in order — and any key points or phrases that are important.

So for *Little Red Riding Hood* it would look like this:

CHARACTERS:
Little Red Riding Hood – young girl
Mother
Big Bad Wolf

Grandma
Woodsman

PLACES:
Kitchen with Mother
Forest – on the path
Forest – off the path
Grandma's cottage

ACTIONS:
Mother sends **Little Red** to visit sick **Grandma** with basket of food.
Little Red wanders off the path to pick flowers.
Wolf asks her what she's doing.
Wolf goes ahead and eats **Grandma** and dresses in her clothes.
Little Red reaches cottage, is confused by **Wolf**.
She says: *Oh Grandma, What Big eyes you have!*
Wolf Replies: *All the better to see you with.*
She says: *Oh Grandma, What Big ears you have!*
Wolf Replies: *All the better to hear you with.*
She says: *Oh Grandma, What Big teeth you have!*
Wolf Replies: *All the better to eat you with!*
Wolf swallows **Little Red** whole.
Woodsman hears commotion, comes in and finds **Wolf**.
Kills **Wolf** and saves **Little Red** and **Grandma**.

These are the bones of the story! Just writing them down can really help you to work out what the important parts are, the pieces that have to be there for the story to be *that* story.

Instead of trying to learn all of the details, or a long script, you can learn what happens, and the order, and that will support you in telling that story. You can also check the bones of the story before you go into ritual to remind you of what you've learned, or if you haven't told the story for a year and just need to jog your memory.

Exercise: Gather the Bones

Your turn! Take the story you chose to work with and write down the bones. Remember, these are:

THE CHARACTERS
THE PLACES
THE ACTIONS/HAPPENINGS

Include any key pieces of dialogue or details that are essential to the story, such as the back and forth between Little Red and the Wolf above, but only the pieces that are key. This should be the bare minimum, remember, just the bones.

Then, the Connections

Once you've learned the bones the next thing to do is to tell the story to yourself, to get a feel for how the pieces are connected.

I find it helps to record it as I go, just on the voice note app on my phone, to keep me from wandering off. But whether you are recording or not, start at the beginning and talk through the story. Start with a phrase like "Once upon a time..." and begin with introducing the main character. As you mention each plot point, add words that help link them together. It might be a sentence describing the motivation of the character, or it might be as simple as "and then she" or "but...". For example:

OPENING: Once upon a time
INTRODUCE MAIN CHARACTER: there was a little girl with a beautiful red hooded cloak.
FIRST ACTION: Her Mother sent her off through the forest to take a basket of food to Grandma, who was ill...

SECOND ACTION: *BUT* Little Red saw some pretty flowers and was distracted from her task...

And so on.

As you tell yourself the story you might find yourself adding in extra details, like the type of flowers, or describing the forest. That's great! Focus on being able to tell yourself the story-bones in order, as connected pieces, and let the details grow as you journey through the story.

Exercise: Making Connections

Give it a go now, before we move on. Practice telling yourself the bones without looking at your notes, and let yourself add in a few details as you go. It's ok to forget things when you try this, just keep practicing getting from the start to the finish. This helps you feel more comfortable with the story and the more relaxed you are, the easier it is to remember!

Finally, the Flavour

One of the best ways to give a story a sense of atmosphere and reality is to imagine you are moving through the story, inside the world, like an invisible companion to the main character.

If you were in the forest with Little Red, and you looked around, what would you see? What would you smell?

Now consider what atmosphere you want to conjure. Do you want the listeners to be comfortable in the forest, or nervous?

Remember that you're weaving magic, so you want to choose the atmosphere to support the magic. If the ritual involves facing and overcoming fears, nervousness could be helpful, so you might mention the shadows, and the cool wind cutting through her cloak. If the ritual was about finding sources of help, then you might want the forest to feel supportive, so you could describe the sunlight falling through the beautiful green leaves, and the soft song of the birds.

For a gentle telling of Little Red Riding Hood, then, I might say this:

> Once upon a time, **in a tiny village on the edge of the ancient forest,** there was a little girl with a beautiful red hooded cloak, **so soft she used to rub it on her cheek for comfort.**
>
> Her Mother sent her off through the forest, **with its tall pine trees that reached dark green needles to the sun,** to take a basket of **freshly baked bread and sweet red wine** to Grandma, who was ill in bed...
>
> As Little Red **walked along the wide, sunlit path,** she saw some pretty flowers, **bright blue in the shadows of the woods**, and was distracted from her task...

Can you see how these are the same bones, just with some extra colour, texture, and tastes sprinkled in, like seasoning?

Exercise: Tell the Story to the Trees

Decide how you want your listeners to feel — you can always change your mind later — and tell yourself the story again, this time describing the landscape, and some of the sensory details. Pick a couple of things for each step of the story.

See if you can add in just one or two details about each character, and about the places that the action happens in. This is where you start to bring the story to life!

You might like to go outside to a space where you'll be undisturbed and tell the story to a tree, or tell it to a potted plant in your home, just to see how it feels. Think about all the senses and include a detail or two about scent or taste, as well as sight, sound, and touch.

If you record yourself then you can always listen back and find out if there are any pieces that you really like, and want to keep as part of the way you tell this story, to add to your notes.

A Note on Scripted Tales

Some stories require specific language, or include specific phrases, such as those that are riddles or traditional teaching tales. You may also decide that you are happier learning a set script, and that is a perfectly valid path to take too. In these cases, or where the phrasing holds particular mysteries, it is important to learn the precise language of important sections, but for our purposes, and especially when you are starting out, an unscripted tale is usually easier. It also supports you in strengthening your memory, and opening up space for adaptation, inspiration, and the magic that happens when you let the story flow in the telling.

Chapter 5

The Bard's Craft – How to Tell a Story

*We travel together, my listeners and I. I point out the
details of the landscape, the grain growing and feathers
falling, cool water a blessing. Tomorrow someone else
will share a tale, softer spoken than I, drawing them
near with gentle words and a gesture or two. Yesterday
the storyteller was deliberately slow. Me? I move.
Dance and theatre have shaped my movements and I
bring that theatrical nature to the tale, expanding the
story like wings spread over us all. Here I am the most
me I can be, with space to be all of myself, and the story
helps me grow.*

How to Tell Stories – Make Them Yours

If you've been seeking out storytellers, you'll have noticed
that each person has their own style of telling tales. Just as
each witch, magician, druid, bard, and ritualist has their own
way of performing magic, storytelling comes from a personal
expression of something magical and so the style has to arise
from the storyteller's nature.

This isn't something you need to worry about *working out*, it
is something that will develop naturally, so the trick is to play
and find your rhythm, your magic in the story.

Like working magic, to tell a story you learn the skills and
the shape, and then you get out of your own way and enter
into relationship with the other beings present. In magic that
might be spirits and gods, and in performance that might just
be a human audience, but in magical storytelling those beings
include the listening humans, the deities and spirits, your divine
self, and the magic itself.

Once you've learned the story enough that you are starting to feel confident, then you begin to share it. Just like in a conversation you naturally respond to the person you are talking to, adjusting as you go, so too in storytelling you "listen" to your audience and follow as much as you lead.

You can begin by telling the stories to the spirits at home if you like, tell them it's an offering and you're experimenting with how to tell it, and you'd love their support. Or you can share with a friend, or at an open storytelling circle — online or in person.

When you're starting out using storytelling in magic it is worth getting comfortable with the story before you bring it into a magical space, and if you can work with another person to hold some of the magical threads then that means you can focus on communicating the story to the best of your ability — and it will work magic for you! As you practice, you'll find it becomes easier to hold both the story and the magic at the same time, so see how you feel as you go.

Here are some things to consider on your journey. Don't worry about getting everything right from the very beginning, there is no perfect way of storytelling, just things to build on and add in over time.

The Practicalities of Being Heard/Seen

When you're working with other people you need to make sure they can hear the parts they are supposed to hear, and see the parts they are supposed to see. This means that you will need to make sure that you are in a position where you can be seen, and where you are directing your voice towards the people listening. This is particularly important when there are people who use lip reading to support their hearing, but needs to be a consideration in any magical working or performance. If the words are important, then they need to reach the audience.

- Take a look at your ritual layout — where will most of the speaking happen? Can you lay out the space so you have your back to them as little as possible? There is a practical reason many pagans work in circles — it aids communication.
- If you're going to be moving around, or if the site is windy, then can you project your voice so the people behind you can hear you?
- If you're reading, have you practiced to make sure you can read it with your face up and the book, paper, or device held low enough that everyone can see your face over it? (Please never hide your face in the book! It muffles your words and cuts you off from the other people present.)
- If you are masked — can you speak clearly through the mask?
- If you're outside or in a large or crowded space, you'll need to be louder than if you're in a small, intimate ritual room, and every extra person will absorb some of the sound, so you may well need to adjust for this too.

Practice projecting your voice so you can be heard without shouting and straining your voice. Imagine you are an actor in a Shakespearean play and need to be heard at the back of the theatre. Stand with your feet firmly on the earth, or feel your connection to the earth. Relax your throat (yawning helps!) and roll back your shoulders to open your chest. Breathe into your belly, using your diaphragm at the base of your ribcage to pull in and push out the air. Speak as though the sound is coming from your belly, or your chest, rather than from your throat.

Remember to warm your voice up beforehand. You can find warm up exercises online, but failing that you can also sing gently to yourself, hum, and make silly noises, like the sounds of sirens and animals, to warm up the muscles of your voice.

Make sure to keep hydrating too, look after yourself!

The Energetics of Being Heard/Seen

If you're feeling shy or nervous, you might be tempted to make yourself smaller, to try to hide a little bit. This brings your energy in and restricts your magic. Notice if you are hunching your shoulders, looking down, or pulling yourself in and take a breath, roll your shoulders back and release as much tension as you can.

Conversely, you might be tempted to overcompensate and make yourself extra big and loud to hide the nerves. This ends up redirecting the magic into appearances, and makes it harder for you to hold the space. If you notice this, then, again, take a breath and as you breathe out, feel your nervous energy sinking into the earth. Let your spirit rest in your body, in the space that is comfortable for you, and feel the support of the earth holding you. Take a moment to ground yourself and find your centre.

People have been telling stories and making magic for as long as there have been people, you've got this. You don't need to be anything except yourself. It is perfectly normal to feel nervous, and perfectly fine if you don't. Just take a breath, rest upon the earth, and let the story begin.

Your Voice

Remember the *Power of the Voice* exercise from Chapter 1? You can use different styles of speaking in order to direct the energy. Obviously, you need to be loud enough for the circumstances, but experiment with telling important parts of the story with your different voices. What happens when you lean in and (stage) whisper? Or speak softly? What about when you use short, sharp words and sounds? You've probably experienced how a sing-song tone can make something sweet or unsettling, depending on the way it is done, so explore the way the energy shifts as you use different ways of expressing things, and ask your listening friends for feedback afterward!

The Acoustics and Spirits of Place

Another piece to consider is the spirits of the place that you are telling your tale in, and you can begin a conversation with them through exploring the acoustics of the space. Beforehand, or while you're setting up, speak or sing to the spirits and listen to how the space responds.

- How is your voice strengthened or softened by the way the space holds you?
- Is there a spot where the echoes become delayed, like someone is replying?
- Is there a spot where the sound is particularly muffled?
- Is there a spot where your voice is lifted effortlessly?
- And how does it feel to be in communion with the spirits here?

Considering the physical qualities of the sound — which you can do by feel, speaking or singing and just noticing what feels good — is part of the process of engaging with the spirits in the physical space. Sound is one thing that is between the physical world and the spirit world, being both manifest and energetic vibrations, so it is a wonderful tool for connecting with the beings and energies of a place.

You can also offer up a song, chant, or short story for the spirits of the place before you begin. I've found that the Fair Folk particularly enjoy poetry about themselves, and both stories and experience tell of how spirits of land, sea, and sky all respond well to song, but any offering of your chosen medium goes down well.

As always, if your preferred language is not spoken, then you can craft your offering through an instrument or AAC to create sounds for you, sign-language, like dancing, is a tangible way of creating energy in the world too, and written pieces can be offered up on paper through fire (please practice fire safety, as always!). In these cases, you can explore acoustics through an instrument, or you can feel or watch for the response in the space as you make your offering.

As Druid and performer Nimue Brown reminded me recently, when you find those sweet spots while investigating the acoustics in a space it can bring you into a magical conversation with the spirits of place.

Your Style

Some storytellers are very theatrical, with big gestures and a lot of physicality to almost "act out" parts of the story on the stage. Other storytellers tell tales like they are sat by a fire, or round a kitchen table, with their listeners, and it is almost conversational. And other storytellers tell stories in particular traditions with dance that is a whole symbolic language, or illustrated "Crankies" and "Kamishibai" (stories on scrolls that are cranked round a frame to reveal the tale, and "paper theatre" — made of pictures that are swapped round to reveal a story step by step).

One key to storytelling is to find what is authentic to you. Consider:

- What are you comfortable with?
- What style makes you happy?
- Would you rather be moving a lot, or mostly still?
- What is possible and comfortable for your body?
- How are you normally in a conversation?
- What skills do you already have?
- Are there traditions of storytelling in your culture, family, or magical tradition that you can draw on?
- How are you feeling in your body today?

These answers can change from day to day, and even story to story. If you are tired and feeling low energy but are normally quite energetic, perhaps today is a day where you move more gently, or sit in one spot instead of moving round the space a lot. Give yourself permission to be yourself, to bring all of your authentic being to the magic.

When you start telling stories, see whose styles you like, and which ones are less appealing to you. Experiment with different styles in front of a mirror or with a recording device, or a friend, and notice how it feels to you to tell your story in different ways.

Try telling a story and getting more theatrical as you go along, until it feels too much and utterly ridiculous for you, and then bring it down, and see how conversational you can make it before it stops feeling like you're telling a tale at all. This is a good way of finding out your current comfort levels, and discovering your personal style.

Confidence

In storytelling confidence comes from being authentically you, and being sure of your material, so the best thing to do is to practice, to find your way of telling the story you've chosen, and to offer it up as a gift.

One thing that is wonderful to remember is the way in which our mistakes and imperfections help our audience to feel an affinity with us as human beings, to empathise with us as people, and thus, to receive the story we are offering them as a gift. Another really useful thing to remember is that they don't actually know which details you've intended to include, so as long as you share the bones, and the emotion of it, and any keys to the ritual work that you're doing, they won't know if you've forgotten something you wanted to include.

Gesture and Embodiment

So, once you've learned your story, made sure you can be seen and heard, experimented with the energy in different styles of voice, and explored your style, perhaps you're beginning to recognise the way in which the telling of a story comes from an embodied place. You are the one sharing the story, so you bring it into you, and share it through your physical existence.

While storytelling is not about acting the whole tale out like a play, gesture can help to bring it into the world, and can add an element of information that allows you to say fewer words, but communicate a whole lot more.

When you're exploring your story, consider, if you were the main character, where would you be looking? If they're about to set out on a long journey, perhaps you gesture out at the hills in the West, and look towards where they would be. If the main character is carrying a basket of goodies, you might crook your arm like the basket is resting there, and your other hand might move like you are picking up flowers and placing them there for safe keeping.

Gestures can be used occasionally to highlight aspects of the story, and if there is an important moment with repetition, you might choose a gesture to repeat, to emphasize that. For example, I tell a story where the hero meets three wise women, and each one blows a horn to call a type of bird. So, I'll make the "horn-blowing" gesture at the relevant point for each one, which reinforces the fact that this event keeps happening. This helps the audience to connect with the story, and it helps relax people, because repetition gives a sense of familiarity, and drawing attention to it helps to both clarify what is happening, and bring the audience deeper.

When you are moving as if you are inside the story, it can help invite everyone else into the same space too, and, along with the relaxation, this helps them to connect with the magic, and to meet the energies you are invoking.

So, as you tell your story, do you feel like there are gestures, or postures, which really highlight a part of the story you want to draw attention to? That can add a sense of touch and texture to the story? Or, as you tell the story, do you feel like you want to move in a certain way, or look in a certain direction?

Allow these movements to arise in the telling, where they feel natural for you.

Costume, Props, and Music

One of the gifts of storytelling is that you don't need props, though they can add an extra dimension and aid in communication, particularly in large rituals. Consider whether you want to add costuming or props to highlight part of the story. Perhaps you are telling the tale of a goddess who is known for a particular colour, in which case you might choose to wear her colours for the event. Perhaps you're telling the tale of a god with an iconic magical object, and having an object to represent it would bring that energy further into the ritual space.

It may be that this isn't practical if you're either telling several stories or performing other parts of a ritual as well as storytelling, but it is worth considering. In magical spaces we can build altars with objects and colours that represent the magic and beings we're calling in, so you might find, like a performer might decorate the stage, you choose to decorate the altar, to give a focal point for those energies.

Likewise, you might choose to include music in the background, or, if you can play an instrument, as part of the story.

With all of these things, it is important to make sure you don't let them get in the way of the story. If the music is too loud, or your costume is distracting, it will make telling and hearing the story harder, so, unless you're working with a very large group that needs bigger, bolder images to be seen, remember that less is often more effective.

Choose Your Language

Just as you choose the words you use to evoke certain moods and energies, if you are telling stories that would have been originally told in a language that is not yours, you might choose to learn some phrases in the language belonging to the story, to connect to its history and culture.

While you're learning the story you might like to explore different translations, to find the nuances that are hard to translate from one language to another, that may not have words for the original concept. One example is the Welsh word *Hiraeth*, which is often described as meaning a kind of longing, or homesickness for a home one cannot return to, but has no direct equivalent in English. Some words you may choose to gloss, and others you may discover give a nuance to the tale, and root it in the magic of its origin. These are worth weaving in, even if they take a bit more practice to pronounce and a little more effort in order to give the context without breaking the flow of the story.

Remember that language has a magic of its own, and so the words themselves carry connections that can bring unexpected gifts. Including some of these words, particularly for us native English speakers who don't often need to consider it, is also a way of acknowledging the culture from which the story has come, and giving some of your energy to supporting it, albeit in a small way.

Give It the Time It Needs

When you tell a story, particularly if you're nervous, you might find yourself rushing. Take a breath and slow down. Give it time for the words to be heard, for the world of the story to build. If you have a very short amount of time, then choose which part of the story is most important and give that time so that your listeners can relax into it. Include enough details that the characters feel like they might be real, but leave space for your listener's imagination to fill in the details.

Let It Be a Conversation

The biggest difference between storytelling and most other art forms is that you are both there with the audience (and the spirits), and the story can change in response to them. You can expand or change details depending on their reactions, pause if they seem like they need a moment, add humour with a raised eyebrow, speed up if they're getting restless. Again, this doesn't need too much thinking or planning ahead, it will arise from the moment as you tell the story if you let yourself be present with the people and respond to their energy, as you would in a normal conversation. As you get more comfortable telling a story you might find that you can feel the energy in the circle shifting with the mood of the tale, and you can lean into that. Feel your way through it. There is no set formula, let it be a conversation, a dance between you, the story, and the listeners.

K.I.S.S.

This chapter has a lot of things to consider when telling a tale, but don't worry.

1. Learn the bones of the tale.
2. Practice telling it and adding details as seasoning.
3. Be with the story as it dances you and the audience.
4. Let the conversation, and the magic, unfold.

In short: Keep It Simple and Sublime (K.I.S.S.)

Exercise: Exploring Your Style

If you haven't already, work through the questions in this chapter, play with the suggestions, and notice what you discover about yourself and your style of storytelling. Pick one new thing at a time to concentrate on and let your style grow. It's normal for this to evolve over time too, so keeping notes can be a lovely way of giving your future self something to look back over and see how far you've come.

Chapter 6

The Craft of Ritual

The story ends but the magic continues, sweeping us deeper into the journey we have heard. The dance of telling and listening has brought us to this moment of choice in the ritual, opened hearts to the magic, and set our minds at ease. We know why we are here; the story has told us where we are going. While our minds mull over the imagery and ideas in the words, our spirits can surrender to healing and transformation in the cauldron of the Goddess who stirs the magic of our circle...

Which Ritual for Which Witch?

If you work within a particular tradition, or if you've picked up a spell-book or grimoire, you may well have ritual scripts. A set of actions and words to do and say, for a specific, magical outcome.

But what happens when you want to work deeply with a particular myth or story that isn't included in the rituals you already have? Or if you want to make magic with people outside of a specific tradition? At an open ritual with people from the local magical community you may find yourself with Wiccans, Druids, Heathens, eclectic modern pagans, psychonauts, occultists, and several others besides. Whose ritual script would you use?! You may find that the scripts you have don't cover the magic that you want to do, or your practice evolves, or perhaps you've never been part of a group with set rituals.

No script? No problem, you can write your own. Often people who are early on in their magical journey will ask "what's a good spell to do X?" or "how should I celebrate Y festival?". Once you know how to construct a ritual you can begin to craft your own spells and celebrations for any purpose you need. Every ritual we have was written by someone, so there's no reason you can't write one yourself.

If you're just starting out in magic, I do recommend exploring folk magic spells, charms, and grimoires as well as writing your own rituals. This is a good way to find magical practices and workings with a proven track record that resonate for you. This can give you powerful practices to incorporate into your rituals, though discernment is required, of course! Not every old folk charm is suitable for today, or for every person. A vegan might decide against using a dried toad charm but instead find a prayer that brings insight, or astrological information on planetary days that inspire the best time to perform the ritual. It's also very important, however, to check modern toxicity information before consuming or burning *anything*, however natural. Be safe!

Traditional correspondences, charms, and spells can be powerful, and, when appropriate ones are found they can be incorporated into a ritual working with a myth. Some even have obvious links to specific deities. If you work with the Norse gods there are Anglo-Saxon healing charms that mention those gods by name, for example, which can stand alone or inspire parts of a ritual based on a Norse myth, strengthening the magic you do. Magic is a practical pursuit, so use what works for you.

The Story of Ritual

Ritual: a structured series of actions including altered states of consciousness, performed with intention for a specific effect, in this case, to cause magic.

There are broader senses of the word "ritual" (some people consider getting their morning cuppa to be a ritual) but for our purpose ritual is specifically performed within the context of a spiritual or magical process. As magic-workers we use ritual to both shift our own states of consciousness and to effect change in the world via "non-obvious" means.

A ritual can be used to help us relax and open enough to talk to our gods and spirits, or it can be used to cast a spell, or a variety of other things, but these things can also be done without ritual. So 1) why use a ritual? And 2) what makes a ritual?

Why Use a Ritual for Your Magic?

Many of us weave our magic into our daily lives with "little rituals" — you might pull a tarot card to receive messages from the Divine powers in your life over breakfast. You might practice grounding in the shower. You might place affirmations or magical glyphs throughout your home so their energy is gently invoked every time you see or say them. And this is the foundation and key to living a magical life. For the sake of simplicity, let's call these "magical practices".

However, *rituals,* as structured series of actions, allow us to do more intense work. For most of us, magical space is not a suitable space to be in constantly, and we need to operate in the "mundane" realm of work and socialising and so on. During ritual we set aside time and space to get our fingers into the mechanics of the universe, where our words and actions have a larger effect than usual, and so it's good to have that contained so an off-hand comment while we're washing up is less likely to manifest in our lives.

Caveat: over time and with a regular practice the division between our mundane lives and our magical lives can fade, but if you don't know how to move deliberately between the two states this can lead to all sorts of muddles in the modern world where the structures to support full-time magic-workers are few and far between. Ritual allows us to experience magical states safely and with support for our ability to be in the "mundane" world. This is why it is important to ground back into your body and fully after any magical work, and to have a strong sense of "everyday" consciousness that you can return to.

Ritual, then, creates a space and time where we can:

- experience deeper connection,
- receive clearer messages,
- and magically effect the world much more strongly.

It also allows us to choose when we are in a magical state of mind, and, over time, helps us to strengthen our skills for moving into and out of magical spaces at will.

What Makes a Ritual?

A ritual, ideally, includes these pieces:

1. An intention,
2. A container,
3. Connection,
4. Inspiration,
5. Transformation.

Let's clarify these.

Ritual Ingredient 1: Intention

An intention: This is where a ritual starts. What is the reason for this ritual? What are you trying to achieve? What magic are you weaving? Without an intention it is very difficult to choose the best shape for it, or to know what transformation you are seeking. So step one is to set your intention. We explored how to clarify and word magical intentions in Chapter 1, "setting" an intention means to both choose an intention, and to get clear that that is what you have decided on. This is what makes an Intention different from a hope.

Exercise: Intention

Remember a time when you felt like something "might be nice", but you weren't really bothered whether you achieved it or not. Now remember a time when you "set your heart on" something, when you decided that you were going to achieve it. These can be small things, like what you wanted to eat for dessert, or bigger things like career choices. The key is to notice the difference between a vague intention, and one you have "set".

Ritual Ingredient 2: A Container

For a ritual to be a time and space set aside from the "mundane" world there needs to be a container, a boundary between ritual-time and non-ritual-time, like the ways you've "marked magical space" to practice the exercises in the book so far. The simplest way to mark these edges is to declare the ritual begun, and to declare it finished, perhaps with lighting and extinguishing a candle. You can also choose clothes or jewellery which you put on to indicate to yourself when you are entering ritual-time, including costume or devotional pieces. One common ritual container you may be familiar with, however, is the act of casting a circle, and taking it down at the end. You can find a simple method of casting a circle in Appendix 1.

Exercise: Containers

What are your favourite ways for marking the start and end of a magical activity? Do you have a prayer you use to open and close with? Do you like to take a breath and remind yourself of your body? Do you have a special place you like to visit, a particular cushion you sit on, a routine where a set time is scheduled for your practice? If you don't know yet, then what do you think might be fun and inspiring for you?

Ritual Ingredient 3: Connection

Once you've decided on what you want to do and entered the container of ritual-time-and-space, it's time to turn your awareness to that connection you have, at the deepest level of your self, to magic. Simply by existing you are part of the web of magic which flows through all things, so this is a process of letting your conscious mind trust in that connection. For you this might be connection to Divine Love, or to Magic as the energy behind life, or it might be to gods or spirits. This is the connection that supports you in whatever you are seeking to transform.

Exercise: Connection

Take a few slow deep breaths and feel the Earth supporting you. On each breath out allow yourself to relax and sink down, out of your thoughts and into the deep part of yourself that is part of the magic of the world. On each breath in, breathe in the supportive energy of the Earth. When you feel ready, turn your awareness up and on each breath out, breathe up and feel your connection with the expansive energy of the stars and sky. Breathe in the possibility and connection from the skies. Feel the Sky energy flowing down into you and imagine it meeting the Earth energy in you. Breathe into this place where Earth and Sky meet, and as you breathe out let yourself relax, holding the energy softly and letting it hold you. When you are ready, release this and settle back into yourself.

Ritual Ingredient 4: Inspiration

Inspiration is where you let yourself be inspired. You may have specific actions and words you've decided on for your ritual, or you may have a structure with space for improvisation. Either way, let the magic that you connect with inspire you and move you. This allows the ritual to become a conversation between you and the Universe.

Exercise: Inspiration

Repeat the connection exercise above so that you are held by the energy of Earth and Sky, and then, resting in this energy, allow yourself to soften and open to the Divine Wisdom carried within. Allow this Wisdom to make itself known in whatever way works for you — images, words, sounds, knowings, movements — and let it inspire you to move or wrap words around it that you can speak softly to yourself. What phrase, image, or gesture comes to you now? When you are ready, release this with a deep breath in and out, feel yourself settle back into the here and now, and send gratitude to the Wisdom and the magic you have connected to. Inspiration happens when the energy flows in and you are moved by it, or recognise and express something in genuine response to it.

Ritual Ingredient 5: Transformation

Finally, with the transformation, there is a change in the energy. You might raise power to direct it toward the goal, you might move the energy in the world toward your goal, you might allow the presence of a deity to bless and change you. All of these are transformations of what is.

Exercise: Transformation

Reflect on the exercises you have just performed. What changed within you as you did them? Did you feel the transformation in the energy? How did you feel before you started, and how do you feel now? Think back over any rituals and magic that you have done, what was transformed? Was it always what you expected?

Ritual Recipe

To recap, then:

1. A ritual needs an **intention** — why are you doing it?
2. Rituals are set aside from other activities so need a **container**.

3. For them to be effective you need to create or find your **connection** to the magic.
4. Allowing for **inspiration** gives space for the magic, your deep-self, or the spirits you're working with, to help and to give you more than just the information in your own conscious mind.
5. And, as a result, there is some kind of **transformation**.

These are also the components of a story-told!

1. You choose your story based on an **intention.**
2. You open and close it, perhaps with phrases like "Once upon a time" and "Happily ever after", which holds it in a **container**.
3. You **connect** to the story, the magic within it, and your audience through presence.
4. You allow for **inspiration** during the telling, to guide the details and the expression of the story.
5. And finally, the characters, the listeners, and the teller experience the **transformation** of energy, and their selves, through the tale told.

Can you see how the act of telling a story, done with intention and presence, can be a magical ritual in and of itself? So, you can tell a story as *part* of a ritual, you can tell a story *as* a ritual, and you can create a ritual *from* a story. That last one is what we're going to do now.

Chapter 7

From Myth to Magic

As the ritual unfolds the story becomes trance, altars become realms, listening becomes action. Guided by the map given to us through the tale, we choose to transform our selves, and we face our own hearts which answer us swiftly. They have already understood through the language of myth, now our dream selves speak to our waking selves, and we make the dream real in the world.

Creating a Ritual from a Story

In this chapter we're going to work through the process of creating a ritual from a myth or story, so you can see how it works and practice the process. Read this chapter all the way through, making notes on anything you want to amend for your ritual, and then perform the ritual, or use the process as a guide to create your own, as you choose.

To Begin – What is your intention?

As discussed, any ritual has a purpose, an intention. What are you seeking to change, honour, or celebrate? I'll take the example I offered in Chapter 1 to illustrate the process here, "to become a better storyteller", tweaked a little.

An intention: *This ritual is to support me in developing my bardic skills for magic.*

I invite you to follow along with this process using this intention. Together we're going to explore how to bring a myth into a ritual, and this process can then be applied to other intentions, and other stories. If this doesn't feel right for you at this time, however, trust your intuition and change it to suit you. You can also look at your affirmations from Chapter 1 or use the process in that chapter to shape a new one.

Once you've decided on your intention, get curious about the pieces you might need to support this. What are your specific challenges to overcome? For my bardic intention, perhaps there is a sense of powerlessness, which leads to resistance to standing up and improving my skills, or taking opportunities offered. For you, if you had the same intention, perhaps your biggest challenge would be a sense of overwhelm at too much to do. Or perhaps it would be fear of being seen by others and judged.

Explore, too, what is your desire underneath the intention? Perhaps it is to be seen and loved. Perhaps it is to share beauty or knowledge. Perhaps it is to gain a skill to advance your career.

Choose a Story – What resonates, what do you need?

Looking at the desire, the challenges, and the intention itself, think over your favourite stories. Is there one that you really love, whose imagery really speaks to you of your intention? Do any of the stories you resonate with deal with the main character achieving something similar in theme to what you desire?

I particularly like the story of Persephone's descent, and there is a journey in there about going from helplessness (she's kidnapped) to claiming her power (she becomes Queen of the Underworld as well as Goddess of Spring), which is a thread that can resonate with any intention that involves overcoming fear and stepping into one's full self. However, my favourite story is the Welsh tale recorded as *Hanes Taliesin*, specifically the part which I know as the *Birth of Taliesin*, where a young boy named Gwion Bach ("little Gwion") is enlisted to help a magical lady, Ceridwen, create a potion to give her son Morfran the *Awen*, which is magical knowledge and divine inspiration all in one.

You can read the full story in Appendix 3, but the short version is that Gwion accidentally drinks the potion and is chased by a furious Ceridwen. They shapeshift into various forms as they run, and eventually she catches and eats him, and he is reborn as Taliesin, the greatest bard who ever lived. This story ties in very well with a desire to become a better storyteller (bard), even down to supporting the work of improving (stirring the cauldron), overcoming the shifting challenges of learning a story, finding a venue, stage-fright, and so on (the chase), and the receiving of divine inspiration (the Awen).

If you're working with a different intention, or this story doesn't resonate for you, you can use the above example as a way of thinking about the stories. Is there a folktale or myth that resonates with you, and reflects the magic you want to do?

The Keys – What are the symbols in the story?
Once we've chosen our story, we read it through. Look for the key symbols and items in it.

In Taliesin's tale one of the central images is the cauldron. Another is the chase, with Gwion shapeshifting into a hare, a salmon, a wren, and a seed, and Ceridwen becoming a hound, an otter, a hawk, and a chicken, in response. And within the Welsh lore there is a symbol for Awen, three lines coming down like three rays of light: /I \

The cauldron is a symbol of transformation, so at this point let's make this the central image for the first part of our ritual, as a pot to put our challenges in, to be transformed into inspiration (through dedication).

There are folksongs that include the shapeshifting chase, such as the traditional *Fith-Fath Song* from Scotland which Damh the Bard does a version of, so they might be worth looking at for inspiration for a chant, or we can find or make images of the animals in the story to represent the skills we're developing in response to the process of strengthening our bardic skills.

The Bones – What is the plot and main components?

Break down the story into key points. What happens at each stage? Which activities feel important? Write them down as bullet points so you can see them laid out in order. Make it as minimal as you can.

- Ceridwen's son needs help, so she decides to make a potion for him, and enlists Gwion to stir the pot while she collects and adds ingredients to it.
- Gwion stirs the pot for a year and a day.
- When it is ready, three drops containing all the magic spit onto Gwion's thumb and he sucks it, leaving the cauldron full of poison.
- Gwion runs, Ceridwen chases.
- He becomes, in turn, a hare, then a salmon, then a wren, then a seed in a farmyard.
- She becomes, in response, a hound, an otter, a hawk, then a chicken.
- She eats him.
- He magically becomes a baby in her belly.
- She gives birth to him and sends him out to sea in a coracle (boat).
- He is found by Prince Elfin, who names him Taliesin and takes him on as his bard.

The Guide – Who is your guide? Who are you mirroring?

Look at the characters in the story. Who goes on the journey you want to take? Who is undergoing the transformation that we are seeking? In this case it is Gwion-Taliesin.

The Support – Who is the power behind the process? Deity? Land? Element?

Are there any deities? Who supports us in this? In Taliesin's tale it looks like Ceridwen is an antagonist, but it is her knowledge that allows for the creation of the potion, her cauldron, her intention. It is she that gathers all the ingredients and supplies what is needed. It is she that tests Gwion, by chasing him, which gives rise to his need to use the gift of Awen he has gained by practicing the magic he now has by shifting shape to escape. And it is she who becomes the cauldron of transformation at the end, eating him and giving birth to him as the newborn bard, once as a mother, and again, finally, as the sea. Throughout the story she is the catalyst, the guiding power, the teacher, and the initiator.

This suggests that we can ask Ceridwen for support and guidance in that role. While she was not named as a goddess in the original story, Ceridwen is often considered to be one by modern pagans and the powerful role she takes in this tale suggests that we can call on her as such.

Crafting the Ritual

Now we have our key pieces — intention, the story bones, symbols (cauldron, animals, Awen), a guide (Taliesin), and support (Ceridwen) — we can piece a ritual together. You can learn the story, or make sure you have a copy of the story that you like to read. Read through the ritual below and make a copy of the pieces you need, amending any words you'd like to change, and gather any tools or items you'd like to have with you. As you'll see below, for this ritual, the cauldron will be represented by an herbal infusion in a cup, and I like to include offerings in thanks for the support of the deities invoked. (See Appendix 2 for my stance on deity work!)

The tools you'll find in this ritual are:

- The story.
- Cup and spoon.
- Herbal tea (in a teapot if desired).
- An offering cup or dish and a drink to offer in thanks to Ceridwen — apple juice, cider, or tea are good options.
- A candle and somewhere safe to put it for Taliesin. (An LED candle is also fine if you cannot burn things. Safety first!)

Creating the Container

Firstly, set up the space you're using and if you know how, you might want to cast a circle or use a specific ritual opening that you would normally. If not, then take some time to prepare yourself in a way that makes sense to you. Get grounded and clear, take some deep breaths, and let go of outside worries.

Next, you'll want to invite the powers that are supporting and guiding you, Ceridwen and Taliesin, to join you. Ceridwen as the Goddess of transformation and source of Inspiration, and Taliesin as a bard who has taken this journey before. This can be as simple as lighting a candle or pouring a nice drink as an offering for each of them and saying:

"Ceridwen, Goddess of transformation and Inspiration, I offer this drink to you and ask that you aid me in my rite."
"Taliesin, great bard who knows this journey well, I offer this light to you and ask that you aid me in my rite."

State your intention. It can be as simple as:

"This ritual is to support me in developing my bardic skills for magic."

To follow the pattern of the story, this ritual working will be in three parts:

- Stirring the cauldron
- The chase and transformation
- Rebirth as Bard

Part 1. Stirring the Cauldron

This part of the ritual is symbolising the support of the Goddess in your journey, where you have to put in the work. You might choose to make an infusion of herbs to drink — choose herbs that are safe for you and also feel magical. (If in doubt, use an herbal tea bag!) For me, apple and cinnamon tea always reminds me of my first big magical retreat, and apple is considered a fruit of the otherworld and knowledge of magic, where cinnamon is traditionally used in ceremonial magic for solar magic, perfect for working with the bard who becomes known for his shining brow.

The cup then becomes the cauldron, the tea the potion.

If you can't make tea in the space you're doing your ritual, make the tea beforehand, and then pour it into the cup in the ritual. Stir the tea mindfully and contemplate the nature of inspiration, which is said to strike more often when we are dedicated to being present for it to turn up.

When we do the work of honing our skills and making time for inspiration, we are inspired more often.

Just like Gwion put in the work, turning up for a whole year, and was rewarded by the Awen choosing him.

Tell the first part of the story, stir your tea, and reflect on this truth. Allow yourself to listen to any guidance on the work you have ahead from Taliesin and Ceridwen.

When you feel it is time, drink the tea.

Part 2. The Chase

This is the part of the story where the change happens. The Goddess tests the would-be bard, and they allow the inspiration that they have gained to guide them and show them how to change themselves.

Tell the chase part of the story, up until Ceridwen becomes a Hawk, stop before Gwion becomes a seed. Reflect on the challenges ahead.

Here is a good point to raise the energy needed to take your magic out into the world. Chanting both raises energy and quiets the conscious mind so we can send our intention into the universe, through the deep self.

Begin with a request to the powers that be:

"Ceridwen, Taliesin, Awen, help me know how to face the challenges ahead as they arise."

Then begin to chant. You might have a chant that you know already that you'd like to use, or you can simply repeat the names of the animals in the chase.

"Hare, hound, salmon, otter, wren, hawk."

Chant these names, allowing yourself to get louder and faster as you go, feel the energy in yourself and in the room shift, and when you feel it is going to burst, finish with one last round:

"Hare, hound, salmon, otter, wren, hawk, seed, hen, BARD!"

Part 3. The Rebirth

Tell aloud the next part of the myth, up to where the babe is floating on the ocean, and imagine you are being gently held in a magical coracle, floating on the sea. Recite an invocation of your bardic self (below is an example you can use). As you say these words reflect on what it means to become what you are, to be a bard:

> "I am the seed of the bard, growing in the cauldron of Awen.
> I am the babe on the waters, carried by the Goddess to my dream.
> I am the bard becoming, blessed by inspiration.
> I am shining with Awen, carrying all that I need."

When you are ready, state out loud:

> "I am (your name), and I am Bard."

Tell the last part of the myth and reflect on what it would mean to you to be a bard, to have those skills recognised by yourself, by your community, in the world.

When you're ready, thank Ceridwen and Taliesin in your own words and say goodbye. Put out any candles lit, and close the space as you would normally. Make note of anything you experienced as particularly powerful or notable, then eat something and do something mundane to give yourself time to integrate the magic.

Ritual Outline

1. Prepare yourself and your space.
2. Invite in Ceridwen and Taliesin.
3. Make your offerings.
4. Stir the tea as a brew in the cauldron and listen to wisdom and guidance on the work ahead.

5. Chant and raise power, to empower yourself to face the challenges.
6. Allow yourself to be transformed by the Goddess, and "reborn" as the bard you are.
7. Recognise your own self.
8. Reflect on being recognised as a bard in the world.
9. Thank Ceridwen and Taliesin.
10. Close the space.
11. Make notes and ground yourself back in your life.

Following the Bard's Inspiration

The words above are not traditional, I offer them to you now as examples for your own use and so you are welcome to use the ritual above as written, to alter parts of it, or to use it as a model for a ritual you might do with a different story and purpose. The same process can be used for group rituals too, of course!

Looking over this chapter, can you see how the process might be used for writing a ritual with a different story or myth?

Allow yourself to be guided by your own understanding and inspiration, and know that the Awen is there for all of us, infinite, abundant, and free flowing. I have heard it said, elsewhere in Welsh mythology, that Ceridwen's son Morfran grew up to be one of the wisest men in King Arthur's court, so we can trust that even though Gwion gained the Awen intended for Ceridwen's son, the Awen is not finite and he had his own journey to take, with its own rewards.

Your Turn

Pick a story you've always loved and read or listen to it. Let its imagery speak to you. Let the beings within it resonate with you. What magic might this story weave in your life? Perhaps you might explore the story from one character's perspective and write a ritual that follows their journey.

You might also choose to follow their journey to support your transformation, or, alternatively, you might hold a ritual that honours something that they've been through, as an offering to them, or as a way of witnessing that for yourself. For example, you could craft a ritual around Ceridwen's experience of the Chase, or one to bring blessings to Morfran, to support him in finding his own wisdom.

What other ways might you work with a myth or story in your rituals?

Exercise: Step-by-Step Ritual Creation – An Outline

1. *What is your intention?*
   Keep it simple and direct so that the magic is focused on one thing.

2. *Choose a story — what resonates, what do you need?*
   Use the exercises throughout this book to help you choose a story that works for you.

3. *What are the symbols in the story?*
   Look for the main images and things that really jump out at you as you go through the story. Notice the ones that really speak to you. You don't need to work with every image!

4. *What is the plot? Find the bones/arc.*
   As in the chapter on learning the story, break it down and consider what makes up *this* story.

5. *Who is your guide? Who are you mirroring?*
   Who is taking the journey and undergoing the changes that you are wanting to conjure in your life and self? What might be a good offering for them?

6. *Who is the power behind the process? Deity? Land? Element?*
   Who, or what, is making things happen in the story? Who instigates or initiates the process? Who holds the space or supports? Consider whether they might be a good being to ask for support in your work. They might be the same as your guide or might be different. What would be a good offering for them?

7. *What are the main parts of the story you want to work with?*
   Again, you don't need to work in depth with every part of the story, some legends get really complex and convoluted, so consider which aspects are really important to your intention for this ritual.

8. *What actions might you choose for each part?*
   Brainstorm as many possibilities as you can. Do you enjoy chanting? Is there a song that fits the action here? Do you like to dance? Is there a gesture you could do? Is there something symbolic that mirrors the activity in the story — like making tea as a mini-potion? Could you meditate on a part of the story, or use visualisation or journeying techniques? Get as many ideas as you can, and then choose actions for the main parts of the story, for the key transformations. Pick things you are comfortable with, that you, or members of your group, have skills in.

9. *What container will you use?*
   How would you like to begin and end your ritual? Do you have a practice that you are familiar with that works well for you? What helps you get in the mood for magic? What helps you to mark the beginning and end of ritual or magical space? If you're not sure, have a look at the practices in Appendix 1.

10. *What tools and materials do you need? What preparation do you want to do?*

   Look over what you've decided and think about what you'll need to do these things, begin gathering what you need together.

11. *How will you move from one part to another? Are there any logistical things which will support your ritual to flow?*

   Once you have the ritual mapped out and you can see the steps, consider how each step will follow on from the previous one. If you're holding an empty cup and need your hands for drumming next, where will you put the cup? And are there any safety issues? If you are lighting a candle, do you have a safe place for it to sit where you won't burn yourself on it?

12. *Does it all feel right to you?*

   Sit with your ritual plan and notice how you feel about it. Does each part feel right? Does the whole ritual sit well with you? Are you excited and happy about it? Or does any aspect feel like it doesn't fit? If you notice a part that sticks out, then explore whether it is worth changing. This is your ritual so it needs to make sense to you. You can use this process in group rituals too. Assuming it goes as planned, consider how the whole ritual, and each part, is likely to be received by the group. Notice what your intuition tells you and adjust accordingly.

A Note on Offerings

I very much work on the principle that it is better to build a relationship with a being before asking them for something, wherever possible, so before you perform a ritual with specific deities then a good practice is to make an altar for them and spend a bit of time making offerings as a welcome gift. Learning their stories is a really good way to start connecting with them and getting to know them, and let what you find in their tales inspire you as to how you might get to know them a bit better. Making an offering at the start of the ritual is a really nice way of giving something to them in thanks for their help, but respect and avoiding a sense of entitlement is the key. If you're not sure, check out Appendix 2 for some suggestions.

Chapter 8

Storytelling Skills in Magic

*The tale is done, the ritual is closed, and once again
I lean on my staff to hike back to the hearth fire. But
the night is not over. Lit by flickering flames we share
songs and stories and insights from our journey. I listen
more than I speak, honouring the gifts offered by the
Awen that flows freely in us all, until, finally, it carries
everyone to their beds and we dream...*

How to Use Storytelling Skills in Magic

As well as telling stories as part of ritual, or creating a ritual
from a story, practicing storytelling also gives you a whole host
of skills which you can use more broadly in ritual and magic.
Here are some key ones.

Skill 1: Different Voices

By exploring using your different voices — whispered, gently
spoken, projected, shouted, and so on — you can find different
ways of expressing other spoken aspects of ritual. You could use
a booming voice to invoke a solar deity, and a soft voice to settle
participants into trance. As you'll have experienced, this has an
energetic and emotional impact on you as well! A softly spoken
chant uses breath differently, and lulls the chanter into a soft trance,
whereas projecting your voice so it resonates around the space
requires more breath, which means you need to hold yourself in
a strong, open posture to get air into your lungs. This posture
allows for the energy to flow and build, it invokes confidence and
increases power. And the sound itself is a different frequency of
energy as well, so the ways in which you use your voice in your
magic can be chosen to enhance the magic you are doing.

Skill 2: Guiding Listeners on a Journey

Whether you are taking a group on a guided visualisation or journeying solo, the process of learning the bones of a story can be applied to the imagery of a meditation, allowing you to put down the paper — or use just basic notes. This helps you to be more present, which increases both the atmosphere and the energy, and removes the need for torches in a night time ritual!

The experience of telling a story is also good practice for guiding a journey through the inner or astral realms and experiencing it at the same time. The more you practice it the more you are able to experience the stories, or journeys, while you guide others through them as it strengthens your skills in holding both the magical experience and the audience's state (and thus what they might need) simultaneously.

Skill 3: Trance Induction

Storytelling involves supporting the transition from activity to receptivity, which is changing states of consciousness, so this helps the development of guiding others, and yourself, from one state to another, in other words, into and out of trance. As you tell more stories you'll discover the rhythms, voices, gestures, phrases, amount of repetition and detail, and so on that support the move in and out of different states of mind. Just as a shift from "conversational" to "storyteller" voice can signal that it is time to let ourselves step into the inner world, the same shift back from "storyteller" to "conversational" can help signal to people that the story is over, or that it is time to return. At the end of a guided journey, I will often switch from the trancey voice to a more directive one, slightly louder and firmer, and closer to my everyday speaking style as I tell people to come back to the here and now. Since they've been following my guidance, this is a very effective way of signalling the return to this realm.

Skill 4: Research

Finding stories to tell and exploring the bones, the symbols, and the beings within is a wonderful way of strengthening your research skills. While it is worth remembering that this will be your personal interpretation of the material, that is a wonderful way to begin or deepen a relationship with deities, archetypes, yourself, and the magic in the world which the stories tell of.

Skill 5: Lore-keeping and Memory Skills

Memory is a skill that can be strengthened, and learning stories is a fun way to give your memory a good work out! In doing so you also gather more knowledge of the lore of your traditions, which supports ritual, magic, yourself, and your community.

Skill 6: Communication

Many of the skills in storytelling are around communication, and this is another skill used in magic. Whether you are communicating with your subconscious, the universe, your gods, the spirit world, or other humans in your ritual space, communication is one way to guide the energy and keep all the participants on the same page.

Skill 7: Clarity

When you distil down the intention for your ritual, or the bones of the story, you are practicing your skills of clarity and discernment — which then support all your magical work!

Skill 8: Ritual Drama

Storytelling is a performance rooted in language, which can be done with only what you have in any moment as an embodied human. Ritual drama, costuming, and so on can be used to help get in the mood, to invoke the energies you're looking for, and to enhance the ritual experience — which makes doing the magic easier as it gets our playful side on board too! Storytelling skills, then, are tools that you can use to enhance the ritual without needing lots of props and such. The ability to encourage an imaginative response means you can "set the scene" with only words if desired or required.

Skill 9: Creating a Journey

The process of creating a guided journey is much the same as the process of telling a story. You choose your key points and symbols and lay them out like the bones of a story, and then weave them together with enough details to keep people focused, and enough space to let them experience what comes through for them. Rather than using someone else's script, then, you are developing the ability to create your own.

Skill 10: Connecting with the Spirits

Story and song are pieces of magic that we can carry with us and offer to both humans and other beings, extended in friendship and care, and offering these to a place, exploring the acoustics and reflections and responses that the place gives in return, is a wonderful practice for connecting with the spirits of that place. You can tell stories to the sea or the trees, or sing or sign in a space and feel it sing with you. You can share a story as an offering of gratitude, or a prayer for support, and step into that back and forth of reciprocity with the world of spirit that we tend to forget is possible. And if you listen carefully, they'll send new stories your way, with wisdom and gifts to guide you along your way.

And More Will Come...

As you practice your storytelling you will find that the subtle skills you develop — such as an intuition for your audience's responses, a sense of how much to elaborate or leave out, when to speed up or slow down, when to speak softly or more firmly, and all the things that you will discover — will enhance your ability to create and lead ritual, and to weave magic for yourself. Your intuition will increase, it supports divination as you expand your understanding of symbols and the language of myth, and the stories themselves become teachers.

Let the process unfold and let the Storytellers of Old, the Bards and Skalds and Grandparents round the fire, guide you.

Chapter 9

Next Steps

The dreaming is done, the circle is open, and all have left. I look round at the empty ritual yurt, fresh sunlight seeping through the canvas. The tale is done, at least for now, but a storyteller's skills are carried with them. The gift of the Bards in whose footsteps I walk are intangible but fill me with a warmth that continues to grow with every tale shared. And I remember that human beings have always shared stories, we shape our world with stories, we understand ourselves and each other with stories. There's a risk here, and a responsibility; to choose the stories we keep alive carefully, to bring growth and love and healing. Resting in my heart are the tales of my gods, of the land, and of magic. I know that I'll continue to share them as blessings and enchantments for the rest of my life... and they bless me with so much in return. We are storytellers, and we are magic.

What Next?

And so they all lived happily ever after...

But the end of the story is not the end of the adventure, nor is the end of our time together the end of your journey. Take a moment to reflect on where you've come from. If you've worked through this book then you have:

- Practiced finding clarity in your intentions and language.
- Written a spell — in the form of an affirmation.
- Explored creating an invocation.
- Learned about different ways to use your voice, spoken and written.

- Considered the way stories are spells.
- Learned methods for choosing stories that will support you.
- Begun to build your story-collection.
- Explored different archetypes and their roles in stories and magic.
- Met archetypes and deities through stories.
- Explored the magic of the Pagan Festivals through story, and of your own land.
- Developed the skills for learning a story.
- Learned how to tell stories without learning a script.
- Learned how to create a ritual from scratch.
- Deepened your understanding of how a story can be transformed into a ritual.
- Performed a story-based ritual.
- And told stories in a magical context.
- Created your own story-based ritual.
- Learned stories and practiced telling them.
- Reflected on how to use the skills you've gained in other aspects of your magic.

So, what next?

The next thing to do is to use these skills!

Just as Witchcraft is a *craft*, a process of doing, so too is Storytelling an act of *telling*. Stories live by being told, by being shared, through whichever medium you choose. When I use the word "storytelling" I'm generally talking about live oral storytelling, and the practice of sharing in person, but there are so many other ways you can share stories if you prefer. Some people dance or sing or write, others crochet or weave objects that represent a tale, which is shared and remembered when the object is discussed. (For example: "That's a beautiful scarf!" "Thanks, I wove it in honour of Ariadne, whose thread guided Theseus safely out of the Labyrinth...").

If you'd like to share more oral stories, however, to tell them or listen or both, then the best way is to find a storytelling circle. There are storytelling festivals where you can watch professional storytellers, and there are informal circles where anyone can practice. These can be both in person and online, so you can join wherever you are in the world. Storytelling also often happens alongside sing-alongs around the fire at festivals, particularly pagan ones, so if you find yourself wishing you could contribute, have a five-minute tale or two to share when it comes round to you.

Another option is to record yourself and share your stories on an audio or video hosting site (such as YouTube), or to livestream them on social media.

You can also set up a local storytelling circle! Chat to local community spaces, bookshops, and cafes that have space for a group to gather and ask if they'll let you use the space in return for donations, or if everyone that comes buys a drink. Invite your friends, put up a post on social media and a poster in a few places in town, and see who turns up. You might only have a couple of people at first, but even if there's just you and the staff, you can tell them a tale! If in person events are impractical for you then there are video conferencing programs, like Zoom, which you can use for an online circle. Either way, have a little explanation prepared for the beginning that you can share, (such as: "Hi, this is a space for anyone who wants to share a story, put your hand up if you've brought a tale to tell.") any guidelines (is it a family space or adults only? Are any topics off-limits? Or would you like people to give a content warning if something might be sensitive? If online, do they need to mute themselves if they're not telling a story?) and a thank you for coming whether they're telling or listening! A story is only half a story if no one hears it so the listeners are as important as the storytellers.

There are other books and courses which you can study to support you in building your skills — find some of these in Appendix 4. These are fabulous for getting ideas to deepen your skills, finding more stories, and exploring the nature of storytelling.

Consider how you'd like to bring the skills you've learned into your magical practice. Do you want to use more affirmations? Are there ways you'd like to add the symbols you find in the stories that speak to you to your altar or practice? Do you have a journal to collect the pieces of magical lore you find in the myths and folk tales? Which story are you feeling called to work with? Which deity do you want to get to know better? Which archetype do you want to bring more deeply into your life?

Experiment with creating rituals based on the stories that call you. Try them out. If you have magical friends, perhaps they'd like to try writing a ritual with you based on a story you tell them.

Have a look at any rituals you've used before. Are there ways you might want to change how you do them now, based on your new skills?

Think about where you might agree or disagree with my model of ritual, and why? You might begin to experiment with changing parts of it and seeing how it works.

Continue using the affirmations, invocations, and intentions you've created in this process for as long as they feel relevant, and change them as needed. Keep notes in your magical journal of any changes you notice, any results, any things that seem odd in some way. Look back periodically and see how your life has changed, and how it has stayed the same. What gifts is the magic of story bringing to you?

Let the stories teach you about yourself and your life. Notice how you feel when you read or listen to them and explore what that feeling is telling you. If you have a strong emotional reaction to part of a story, positive or negative, then make a note of it and continue. Once you've finished the tale reflect on why you responded to that part. Do you feel better about it now you know how the story ends, or worse, or the same? Why did that particular part matter to you? What does the unfolding of events in the story tell you about what you need to do now? Or what you need to not do?

Let the stories teach you about magic. When you explore a myth that has strong magical themes then you might find that it contains inspiration about how to deepen your magical practice. Allow inspiration to flow and notice what happens.

You are writing the story of your life and your magical journey. As such, you have joined the path of the Bard, the Skald, the Storyteller. You are in good company, and wherever you go, wherever you stay, you have picked up the power of stories and that is something no one can take away from you.

May your memory be strong, your voice be clear, and your story be blessed.

I'll see you on the storytellers' road.

Appendix 1

Foundational Magic Skills

This appendix includes some very basic starting points for magical practice, if you'd like to learn more, I offer in-depth courses at The Enchanted Academy (or TEA for short, because TEA is magic!).

Visualization (and Other Senses)

In magic, one of the main tools we use is our imagination, coupled with intention to direct energy and communicate what we desire to the gods (however you see them). This is often called "visualization". Visualization is not just picturing things in your mind, but involves imagining what you are doing — moving energy, a landscape you are journeying through, the outcome of a spell — with as many senses as you can. If you are not a visual person then it is absolutely OK for those senses to not be visual. Use the senses that work best for you, and build the others with practice, if you can, to support your magic further.

To visualize, then, use as many imaginative senses as possible to create what you desire in your mind, and intend that it is really happening. The difference between "mere" imagination and visualization in this sense is like the difference between thinking you are awake when you're dreaming, and knowing you are awake. Play with it and notice when it feels "real". Remember that feeling and, as you practice, bring that feeling to mind when you are doing magic. With practice it becomes easier and more consistent.

As you do this, relax and approach it with a sense of playfulness, building these skills will make it your magic more effective, but just having a clear intention will move energy, and, as discussed in Chapter 1, the vibrations of your words and gestures are putting the magic you want into the world as well.

Energy – What Is It?

"Energy" in a magical context is a vague term, so the easiest way to explain it is to show you.

Take a nice slow breath, and as you breathe out, let yourself relax.

If you can, shake your hands and then bring them slowly together.

Rub your palms together briskly, breathing slowly and deeply.

Slowly bring your hands apart a little way and move them closer together and further apart.

Notice what you feel.

Do you feel a tingle, or a pressure like a cushion of air, or the resistance of two poles of a magnet being pushed together?

That sensation is a good experience of what energy feels like.

Energy is a term used to describe the power which we use to cause change in the world through magic. It can also be the lifeforce that moves within us, constantly being renewed, the vibrations that flow through the universe, the feeling of fieriness that rises when we're passionate. All of these can be used for magic, to change the patterns of the universe and create a new reality.

How to Cast a Simple Circle

In this book I mention creating a container to mark the beginning and end of your rituals. One common technique in paganism and Western Magic is to "cast a circle". This means to draw a circle (or, better, a sphere) of energy around your working space, and then to remove it at the end.

Creating an energetic container gives you both a boundary of time and space, among other benefits such as protection and focus.

To support the process you can mark the circle on the floor with rope, chalk, flower petals, or anything else you choose, though be aware of how you'll clean it up afterward!

Then draw that boundary line in the air with your finger, visualizing energy like light rising from the earth beneath you, up through your body, and out through your finger, marking the edge of the circle and growing up and down, curving into a sphere around you.

When you are done, draw the circle backwards, starting where you ended and tracing it round in reverse, imagining the energy being gathered back into your finger and flowing back into the earth until the sphere is gone.

You can also use a wand or a ritual knife to draw the circle, say words describing what you're doing and telling the circle what it is for, draw symbols such as pentagrams in the cardinal directions, call on the elements or beings that you're working with to hold the circle, and many other things, but at its most basic casting a circle is as simple as drawing the energy like a curtain around you.

How to Ground

Grounding is a really important practice of releasing excess energy and bringing yourself back to your everyday consciousness.

The simplest method is to breathe in, visualizing any excess energy gathering in your core, and then breathe out and visualize it sinking into the earth to be released, feeling your feet or butt on the floor (or your seat). Focusing your feeling in your feet or butt brings you back down into your body and reminds you to be here and now.

You could also reach down and touch the earth, walk barefoot outdoors, eat something crunchy and salty, or do something really mundane, like washing the dishes.

Cleansing Practices

Just like we wash the dirt off our hands before we make food, it's good to wash the energetic dirt away before making magic. You can do this simply by washing your hands and face with cool water and the intention of clearing away energetic dirt. I was taught to use rose water, or water with a pinch of salt added, for extra cleansing power. You can also bless the water by holding your hands over it and visualizing it filled with bright white or golden light, or with a few words asking the water to lend its cleansing power to you.

Appendix 2

Gods and Spirits

You do not need to believe in gods or spirits to use this book. You can approach them as archetypes, or anthropomorphic representations of forces in the world, or psychological constructs. As a polytheist I work with deities as independent spirit beings, bigger than us and interested in humanity, and I've found that treating them as such has better results for me than treating them as archetypes, though your experience may be different. Whether they are independently "real" or not, when I approach them with respect and as though they are as real as I am, my mind engages better and they respond better. I invite you to consider treating any gods you choose to work with as though they are real, they care, and that you can build a working relationship with them and see what happens.

In a lot of cultures the gods are our ancestors, our relatives, and, just like our human relatives, we may not want to work with all of them, and they may not all want to work with us, but as you explore their stories you may find that some of them offer support.

If you're just telling their stories then that in itself can be a way of honouring them, through remembering them, but if you're asking them to support your magic then it's good to know them a bit better!

Relationship Building

When working with deities in an ideal world it is good to have some kind of relationship built up before you start asking for things, though we often turn to deities in times of need.

If you're working with a specific deity's myth, then while you are learning their story is a good time to start building a relationship. The process of finding their story and working with it to get to know them is, in itself, part of the process, much like chatting to a new friend in order to find out their likes and dislikes, listening to the stories of their life.

An altar is a magical working space, and in that space you can create a shrine to "house" the deity, whether as a guest or as a long-term resident. A shrine is a space dedicated to a deity or spirit (like a saint) where they can be present, a space with imagery and objects that represent the being you are making space for in your life and home. Choose a safe space where they won't be disturbed and add an object or two that remind you of them. You might like to include a cup for offerings of drinks, or a candle or incense to light for them.

Offerings are much like feeding your guest, to make sure they are comfortable and have what they need. They also work on the principle of reciprocity — if you look after them, they will likely look after you. Key to all of this is to adopt an attitude of building connection with respect rather than entitlement.

Like with humans, what you put into a relationship is often proportional to what you get back, and of a similar kind. Invite them in as a guest, and if it is only a temporary partnership then when your time together is over, say farewell. If you choose to work with them again in the future, you may well find that they remember you kindly too.

Appendix 3

The Birth of Taliesin

In the mountains of Eryri, upon the shores of Lake Bala, lived the lady Ceridwen and her two children. Her daughter was beautiful and clever, but her son Morfran was so ugly people called him "utter darkness", and so stupid that she feared he would never make his way in the world. She decided to use her magic to make him a potion to grant him the Awen, Divine wisdom and inspiration. She commissioned a great cauldron which was placed beside the lake in a hut where a fire could be kept burning beneath it. She enlisted the aid of the orphan, Gwion Bach, and his old, blind guardian Morda, to stir the pot and tend the fire for the time that it would take to make the potion.

For a year and a day Gwion stirred the pot and Ceridwen gathered the herbs for the brew at the correct times, adding them with the correct words, waiting patiently for the magic to come to fruition. The day came when the brew was ready and Ceridwen went to fetch her son from the house. In those last few moments the potion bubbled, and the bubble burst, and the potion spat three drops containing all the magic of the cauldron onto little Gwion's thumb. He yelped from the burn and immediately, without thinking, put his thumb in his mouth to soothe the pain. As the three scalding drops slipped down his throat he became inspired. Gwion gained the knowledge meant for Morfran, and he knew his life was in danger from the mother whose son had lost his way in the world.

Little Gwion ran. Behind him the potion left in the cauldron had turned to such dangerous poison that it cracked the cauldron and poured across the land, killing all in its path. When Ceridwen discovered what had happened she was furious and, seeing that Gwion had run, she gave chase.

He ran fast but she ran faster, so he took his new knowledge and transformed into a hare. Ceridwen became a greyhound and drew nearer. Gwion saw the river up ahead, so he leapt into the water as a salmon. Ceridwen became an otter and drew nearer still. Gwion leapt into the air and became a wren. Ceridwen followed as a falcon and plucked a feather from his tail. Finally, Gwion saw a farmyard below, littered with grains of wheat, so he curled up tight and became a grain, dropping to the ground. Ceridwen landed and became a great, black hen. One by one she ate every grain in the yard.

When she returned home as a woman once more, however, she found that the magic had transformed the seed of Gwion in her belly into a child. For nine months she carried him and when he was born she loved him. But the baby could not stay there, so she wrapped him in an oilskin and placed him in a coracle on the ocean waves.

It was May eve and Prince Elfin, the unluckiest prince you ever did meet, was fishing from the weir. It was said that any who caught a salmon on that day would have good luck for the coming year and Elfin was determined to turn his luck around. Thus far he had caught a minnow, half a crab and an old boot. The sun was beginning to set when his line caught something large, heavy enough to be a great fish, and Elfin pulled it to shore! When he found only an oilskin bag he was not surprised. Unwrapping the contents, however, revealed something he had never expected to see, a baby that stood up, shining with a bright light, and speaking as eloquently as if he were fully grown.

"Prince Elfin," the baby said, "take me into your family and you will never again be unlucky, for I am the greatest bard that ever lived and I will turn your fortunes around."

Elfin did not need telling twice, and so the baby was adopted and named for his shining brow, Taliesin. Sure enough, Taliesin did transform Elfin's fortunes from then on.

Taken from "Gods and Goddesses of Wales" (Moon Books, 2018), with minor edits.

Appendix 4

Recommended Reading

Gods and Goddesses of Wales – Halo Quin (Moon Books, 2015)

Folktales, Faeries, and Spirits – Halo Quin (Moon Books, 2022)

The Bardic Handbook: The Complete Manual for the 21st Century Bard – Kevan Manwaring (Gothic Image, 2006)

The Way of Awen: Journey of a Bard – Kevan Manwaring (O Books, 2010)

The Storyteller's Way: A Sourcebook for Inspired Storytelling – Ashley Ramsden and Sue Hollingsworth (Hawthorn Press, 2013)

Our Secret Territory: The Essence of Storytelling – Laura Simms (Sentient Pub., 2011)

Neo Pagan Rites: A Guide to Creating Public Rituals That Work – Isaac Bonewits (Llewelyn Pub., 2007)

Discover an ever-evolving page of resources to help you on your journey in the storytelling section at www.haloquin.net/resources.

About

Halo Quin

Halo is a lifelong lover of magic. She is a devotee of Freya and the Faery Queen, a lover of the Welsh land and gods, a storyteller, philosopher, and a sensual witch working to (re) enchant the world.

As a storyteller, Halo has told tales across Britain, worked in living history as an iron age bard, created a delightful "one-woman-many-goblin" show; The Goblin Circus, and runs Fables, a local storytelling circle in her home county of Ceredigion, Wales. She specialises in myths, legends, and fairytales, and is often seen wandering an event with a gryphon in tow.

Magically speaking, Halo is an initiated Feri witch who has trained and taught within Reclaiming witchcraft, a Druid in the Order of Bards, Ovates, and Druids, and has co-created and facilitated seasonal rituals for the local pagan community for almost two decades so far. She is the creator of *The Enchanted Academy* (or TEA for short) for pagan classes and witchy magic, including the *Crimson Coven* for embodied magic and pagan sacred sexuality, and co-leader of the *Star Club* for ceremonial magic.

Oh, and her PhD was in the Philosophy of storytelling. You can, of course, find all these things and more at www.haloquin. net.

Readers of ebooks can buy or view any of these bestsellers by clicking on the live link in the title. Most titles are published in paperback and as an ebook. Paperbacks are available in traditional bookshops. Both print and ebook formats are available online.

Find more titles and sign up to our readers' newsletter www.collectiveinkbooks.com/paganism

For video content, author interviews and more, please subscribe to our YouTube channel.

MoonBooksPublishing

Follow us on social media for book news, promotions and more:

Facebook: Moon Books

Instagram: @MoonBooksCI

X: @MoonBooksCI

TikTok: @MoonBooksCI